SOPWITH CAMEL
VS
FOKKER Dr I

Western Front 1917–18

JON GUTTMAN

First published in Great Britain in 2008 by Osprey Publishing,
Midland House, West Way, Botley, Oxford OX2 0PH, UK
443 Park Avenue South, New York, NY 10016, USA

E-mail: info@ospreypublishing.com

A CIP catalogue record for this book is available from the British Library

ISBN: 978 1 84603 293 6

Edited by Tony Holmes
Page layout by Myriam Bell
Cover artwork, cockpit and armament scrap views by Jim Laurier
Three-views by Harry Dempsey
Battlescene by Mark Postlethwaite
Index by Alan Thatcher
Typeset in Adobe Garamond and ITC Conduit
Originated by PDQ Digital Media Solutions
Printed in China through Bookbuilders

08 09 10 11 12   10 9 8 7 6 5 4 3 2 1

For a catalog of all books published by Osprey Military and Aviation please contact:

NORTH AMERICA
Osprey Direct, c/o Random House Distribution Center, 400 Hahn Road,
Westminster, MD 21157, USA

E-mail: info@ospreydirect.com

ALL OTHER REGIONS
Osprey Direct UK, PO Box 140 Wellingborough, Northants, NN8 2FA, UK

E-mail: info@ospreydirect.co.uk

Osprey Publishing is supporting the Woodland Trust, the UK's leading woodland
conservation charity, by funding the dedication of trees.

www.ospreypublishing.com

Cover art

Arguably the second most famous clash between the
Sopwith Camel and Fokker Dr I occurred on 20 April
1918, when Jagdstaffel 11 took on No. 3 Sqn RAF.
During the course of the engagement Rittm Manfred
Freiherr von Richthofen killed Maj Richard Barker and
brought down 2Lt David G. Lewis as a POW, thus raising
his score to 80. In the same fight, American 1Lt Lloyd A.
Hamilton of No. 3 Sqn RAF fired 300 rounds at a blue
triplane and saw it descend in a spin. Although his victory
claim remained unconfirmed, Hamilton was ultimately
credited with ten successes flying with No. 3 Sqn RAF
and the 17th Aero Squadron, USAS, before being killed
by ground fire on 24 August 1918. Fellow American
2Lt M. Curtis Kinney also claimed to have taken a fleeting
shot at the Red Baron before being fired upon by 'a green
and white triplane' on 20 April. Kinney escaped, but
his 'demise' may have been erroneously credited to his
assailant, Ltn Hans Weiss of Jasta 11. (Artwork by
Jim Laurier)

German ranks	RFC/RAF equivalents
Rittmeister (Rittm)	Cavalry Captain
Hauptmann (Hptm)	Army Captain
Oberleutnant (Oblt)	Lieutenant
Leutnant (Ltn)	Second Lieutenant
Offizierstellvertreter (OffzSt)	Warrant Officer
Vizefeldwebel (Vzfw)	Sergeant Major
Feldwebel (Fw)	Sergeant
Unteroffizier (Uffz)	Corporal
Gefreiter (Gfr)	Private First Class
Flieger (Flgr)	Private

CONTENTS

INTRODUCTION

Amid the ongoing quest for aerial superiority during World War I, two aircraft types acquired a measure of lasting mythic fame above and beyond their actual achievements. Both rotary-engined fighters, the Sopwith Camel and the Fokker Dr I triplane were relatively slow for their time, but were regarded as the most manoeuvrable machines to achieve production during the conflict. They were also the classic pair for a tight, evenly matched dogfight at close quarters.

In actuality, the Camel's status as having scored the most victories of any single fighter during the war is largely founded upon all-too-frequent overclaiming on the part of its pilots and overcrediting on the part of its squadrons. Meanwhile, the Dr I's impact on the aerial struggle was delayed by early accidents due to poor quality control, and subsequently handicapped by the chronic seizing up of its rotary engine during the summer of 1918 – which, fortunately for the Germans, coincided with the emergence of a superior successor, the Fokker D VII.

Nonetheless, both aeroplanes occupy legitimate places in the history of combat aircraft development. The Camel was Britain's first production fighter with twin machine guns, while the Fokker triplane has the ironic distinction of being the first production fighter in history with a cantilever wing structure that did away with external bracing, and made the monoplane practical.

In the years following World War I, the two fighters' actual historical merits became enshrouded in myth, primarily thanks to their association with the most familiar name to emerge from the conflict – Manfred Freiherr von Richthofen, immortalized to posterity as the Red Baron. The facts are that at the end of August 1917 von Richthofen, who was then the highest scoring ace of the war and commander of Jagdgeschwader (fighter wing) I, also known as JG I to the Germans and the 'Flying Circus' to the British, became the first pilot to receive a Fokker triplane. Soon after taking delivery of his Dr I, von Richthofen also became the first pilot to claim a victory with it. He went on to raise his tally to 80 on 20 April 1918, his final victims being the last two of eight Sopwith Camels that fell to his guns.

The next day, during another run-in with No. 209 Sqn, Royal Air Force (RAF), von Richthofen was killed while pursuing a Camel behind Allied lines – either by another Camel flown by Canadian ace Capt A. Roy Brown, or by Australian ground troops. For decades, conventional wisdom favoured Brown, sealing the classic duel between Dr I and Camel in the popular memory, in spite of more recent evidence suggesting that the bullet that killed the Baron more likely came from the ground.

The brothers von Richthofen – Lothar, at left, and Manfred beside Fokker Dr I 114/17. Both holders of the Orden Pour le Mérite, they had short, violent careers in Fokker triplanes. Both have more than one claimant for having shot their Dr Is down. (Greg VanWyngarden)

As if that was not enough, the struggle between a dashing 'World War I flying ace' and a certain red triplane was branded into the American psyche through the nostalgic fantasies of a cartoon dog, periodically sallying forth in his 'Sopwith Camel' – or at least on the roof of his doghouse – against the 'Bloody Red Baron' in Charles M. Schultz's comic strip *Peanuts.*

Besides 'Snoopy and the Red Baron', Britons, who tend to remember World War I better than do their American cousins, have the additional legend of the 48-victory ace Werner Voss, the second German to fly a Fokker triplane, whose death on 23 September 1917 came after a spectacular ten-minute fight, mostly alone, against a flight comprising some of the best fighter pilots in the Royal Flying Corps (RFC). As far as the British are concerned, Voss and the Fokker triplane achieved as much immortality in death as did von Richthofen, even though his adversaries that day were flying SE 5as, not Camels.

In a way, posterity is indebted to these legends for keeping general interest in World War I aviation alive. The price of such remembrance, however, is that more people remember the fables than the facts. As is so often the case, anyone interested enough to delve into the truths behind the legends might find them less simple, but perhaps more interesting.

When the Great War broke out in early August 1914, the aeroplane had already seen its first use in the reconnaissance and bombing roles, but by the end of August the first attempts at aerial combat had occurred. With the emergence in the summer of 1915 of the Fokker E I, with synchronized interrupter gear that stopped its machine gun from firing whenever a propeller blade was in front of the muzzle, the quest for control of the skies over the frontline began in deadly earnest. What followed was

Capt Arthur Roy Brown of No. 209 Sqn RAF stands beside his Clayton & Shuttleworth-built Sopwith Camel B7270 at Bertangles. His tenth accredited victory, allegedly over Rittm Manfred Freiherr von Richthofen on 21 April 1918, made him part of the Red Baron legend, although the current prevailing view favours Australian groundfire as the more likely cause of the German ace's demise. (Rod Filan)

Photographed during a visit to Charles Donald in Union, New Jersey, on 14 February 1974, Oliver Colin Le Boutillier, formerly of No. 209 Sqn RAF, poses beside a painting of the Red Baron's last combat, showing Le Boutillier's own Camel at upper right. (Charles Donald Collection via Jon Guttman)

a succession of fighter aeroplanes, ranging from the progressively refined to the radical and even bizarre, all meant to get the advantage in performance and firepower over their adversaries.

The Camel was in the progressive category, with a pedigree that could be traced back to the Sopwith Tabloid racer of pre-war 1914, and readily seen in its martial predecessors, the 1½ Strutter, Pup and Triplane. Apart from its twin-gun arrangement, structurally the Camel was quite conservative – a wire-braced wood and canvas biplane typical of its time.

The Fokker Dr I, on the other hand, was primarily built to satisfy a requirement drawn up in reaction – one might well say overreaction – to the performance of the earlier Sopwith Triplane, yet its wood box cantilever wing cellules represented the structural trend of the future. For all that, though, circumstances, not all of which were unavoidable, doomed the Fokker triplane to a limited production run and a mere three-month period of strategic prominence, whereas the earlier Camel would outlast it and remain a mainstay of British air power right up to the Armistice.

Significantly, the two fighters would meet most often amid the last significant German bid to win the war, known as *Die Kaiserschlacht* ('Imperial Battle'). Therein, too, would lie the myth of their playing decisive roles in the pivotal struggle, disproportionate to the roles they actually played.

CHRONOLOGY

1916

30 May First prototype Sopwith Triplane completed.

July First Sopwith Pups and Triplane prototype arrive at No. 1 Wing Royal Naval Air Service (RNAS) at Dunkerque.

December Sopwith completes prototype Sopwith F 1.

1917

June In response to the Sopwith Triplane, Inspektion der Fliegertruppen orders all German aeroplane manufacturers to submit triplane fighter designs. No. 4 Sqn RNAS receives first Sopwith F 1 Camels.

11 July After his V 4 prototypes impress Idflieg, Anthony Fokker begins work on pre-production F I triplanes.

28 August Fokker F Is 102/17 and 103/17 delivered to Jagdgeschwader I and allotted to Rittm Manfred Freiherr von Richthofen, JG I's commander, and to Ltn Werner Voss of Jasta 10.

1 Sept Rittm Manfred Freiherr von Richthofen, flying F I 102/17, scores first Fokker triplane victory – an RE 8.

3 Sept Von Richthofen brings down a Pup while Voss, probably flying F I 103/17, shoots down a Camel.

10 Sept Ltn Voss, in F I 103/17, downs two Camels and claims two more the next day.

15 Sept Oblt Kurt Wolff is killed in F I 102/17 by a Camel flown by Flt Sub-Lt Norman Miers Macgregor of No. 9 Sqn RNAS.

19 Sept Nos 70 Sqn RFC and 10 Sqn RNAS carry out first organized ground-attack missions by Camels, against German trenches and troop positions along the Ypres front.

23 Sept After a spectacular one-man dogfight with SE 5as of Nos 60 and 56 Sqns RFC, Ltn Voss is killed in F I 103/17 by Lt A. P. F. Rhys Davids of No. 56 Sqn RFC.

October Fokker Dr Is delivered to JG I and other units.

2 Nov After several cases of wing failure, two of them fatal, Idflieg withdraws all Dr Is pending investigation.

December Deliveries of Dr Is with improved construction procedures resume.

German soldiers turned the tables on Clayton & Shuttleworth-built Camel B7230 of No. 8 Sqn RNAS as it was strafing them on 10 March 1918, bringing it down intact and taking its pilot, Flt Sub-Lt K. D. Campbell, prisoner. (George H. Williams Collection via Greg VanWyngarden)

1918

13 January Ltn Werner Steinhäuser of Jasta 11 scores first Fokker Dr I victory – a balloon – of 1918, but Ltn Eberhardt Stapenhorst is brought down by ground fire and his Dr I 144/17 falls into British hands intact.

3 February Flt Cdr R. R. Winter of No. 9 Sqn RNAS is credited with first Dr I shot down by a British fighter in 1918, although Germans actually lose none. Winter is subsequently killed, the only Camel loss that day, but Dr I pilots of Jasta 26 claim five.

21 March Fokker Dr Is, equipping elements of JG I, JG II and JG III, are the best German fighters available as the *Kaiserschlacht*, Germany's last great offensive, commences with Operation *Michael*, focused around Amiens.

April A peak quantity of 171 Dr Is operating over the Western Front.

5 April Germans cancel Operation *Michael*.

9 April Germans commence Operation *Georgette*, a new offensive in the Lys River area.

Airmen of No. 3 Sqn AFC examine the remains of von Richthofen's Dr I 425/17. The aeroplane was recovered largely intact, but souvenir hunters made short work of it. (Greg VanWyngarden).

20 April Manfred von Richthofen downs two Camels, bringing his total to 80.

21 April Manfred von Richthofen is killed – probably by ground fire – while fighting with Camels, and his Dr I 425/17 comes down in British lines.

29 April Amid British counterattacks, Germans cancel Operation *Georgette*.

18 May First Fokker D VIIs arrive at Jasta 11, which begins process of passing its Dr Is to other units.

27 May– 12 June Germans launch Operation *Blücher-Yorck* and its follow-up, *Gneisenau*, in the Aisne sector between Soissons and Reims. The primary opposition is French and American, with fewer occasions for RAF Camels to fight steadily diminishing numbers of Fokker Dr Is.

June–July Rotary engine seizures, mainly due to failure of castor oil substitute lubricant in summer heat, ground entire *Staffeln* squadrons of Dr Is as Fokker D VIIs replace them.

DESIGN AND DEVELOPMENT

SOPWITH CAMEL

The Camel's genesis harkened back directly to the Sopwith Tabloid racer of pre-war 1914, a boxy looking, compact, single-bay biplane of wood and canvas, whose wing cellule was held together by cross-braced wire cables – a basic formula that would characterize most Sopwith designs for the rest of the war. Although the Tabloid and a floatplane derivative called the Baby saw service as scouts in the conflict's early years, Thomas O. M. Sopwith's first true fighting machine was a two-seat reconnaissance-fighter and bomber.

Co-designed with Herbert Smith, armed with a single 0.303-in. Vickers machine gun fitted with Sopwith-Kauper interruptor gear, firing forward and a Scarff ring-mounted Lewis gun aft, the aircraft was named for its W-shaped cabane strut arrangement. The 1½ Strutter was passed by the Sopwith experimental department on 12 December 1915, and it would soon be joined by a smaller single-seat derivative based on a lightweight machine (powered by a 50hp Gnome rotary engine) that had been designed in the autumn of 1915 by test pilot Harry Hawker. Impressed by the sprightly performance of 'Hawker's Runabout', Sopwith and his staff worked on a more robust military version to be powered by an 80hp Le Rhône engine.

Cleared for testing on 9 February 1916, the Scout, as it was officially called, made an immediate impression on the Admiralty and everyone who flew it. Its maximum speed was 110mph at 6,500ft, it could climb to 10,000ft in 12 minutes and it

combined ease of handling, sprightly manoeuvrability and good cockpit visibility, all in one of the most nicely balanced and aesthetically pleasing aeroplanes of the war.

The RNAS put in its first order in April 1916, and when MajGen Hugh Trenchard of the RFC read a copy of the Admiralty's report, he pencilled in a concise comment of his own – 'Let's get a squadron of these'. It was another RFC officer, Col Sefton Brancker, who is credited with declaring, upon spotting a Scout alongside its two-seater forebear 'Good God! Your 1½ Strutter has had a pup'. Despite official efforts to discourage it, the delightful new fighter soon became universally known by that name.

By the time the first Pups arrived at No. 1 Wing RNAS at Dunkerque in July 1916, the prototype of another variant was joining them for frontline evaluation. Completed on 30 May 1916, Sopwith Triplane N500 combined the Pup's fuselage with three sets of narrow-chord, high aspect ratio wings that gave the pilot a better view from the cockpit, a faster climb rate and superior manoeuvrability to the Pup's. So capable was the Triplane that whilst flying N500 on 1 July Flt Lt Roderic Stanley Dallas of No. 1 Wing's 'A' Sqn drove a German two-seater down out of control south-west of St Marie Capelle. On 30 September the Australian-born Dallas repeated that performance on a German fighter.

Even with two first-class fighters in production, Tommy Sopwith was not one to rest on his laurels. For all their virtues, both the Pup and Triplane had a weakness in the slow rate-of-fire of their single Vickers guns when fitted with Sopwith-Kauper gear. This became a real problem when the Germans introduced the Albatros D I and D II, whose twin synchronized machine guns gave them nearly triple the Sopwiths' rate-of-fire. In December 1916, while 'A' Sqn (redesignated No. 1 Sqn RNAS) was fully equipping with Triplanes, Sopwith, together with R. J. Ashfield, Herbert Smith, F. Sigrist and Harry Hawker, completed the prototype of their own twin-gun fighter – the F 1 – which emerged for its first test flight on the 22nd.

Designed in the autumn of 1915 and powered by a 50hp Gnome rotary engine, this aircraft, which was originally built as a runabout for Sopwith test pilot Harry Hawker, became the basis for the Pup, Triplane and Camel. (Museum of Flight Peter Bowers Collection)

11

Initially called the Sopwith Scout by the RNAS, the aircraft became better known as the Pup. N5180 was an early naval example. (Museum of Flight Peter Bowers Collection)

OPPOSITE
Sopwith F 1 Camel B3833 of Flt Sub Lt Norman M. Macgregor, No. 10 Sqn RNAS, based at Droglandt in September 1917. Macgregor brought this aircraft with him from No. 6 Sqn RNAS, and it is reconstructed here in 'B' Flight markings in September 1917, before 'Naval 10' adopted flamboyant bands of white and red, black or blue, depending on the flight, on the forward fuselage. On 15 September 1917, Macgregor sent a Fokker triplane down out of control for his fifth of an eventual seven victories. Unlike most 'out of control' claims, Macgregor's turned out to be genuine, as he had destroyed the first operational Fokker triplane, F I 102/17, and killed Jasta 11's commander, 33-victory ace Oblt Kurt Wolff.

The F 1 had a shorter, deeper fuselage than the Pup, with the engine, cockpit and guns concentrated within the foremost seven feet of its fuselage. To facilitate production, Sopwith eliminated the dihedral on the one-piece upper wing and compensated by doubling the dihedral of the lower one to five degrees. The twin Vickers machine gun installation was partially covered by a fairing that sloped upward from the nose, and which was initially thought to protect the pilot from the slipstream effect suffiently to make a conventional windscreen unnecessary.

Similar though it may have been in construction, the F 1's altered configuration gave it a pugnacious appearance and equally aggressive flight characteristics that differed radically from those of the docile Pup and manageable Triplane. The first F 1 was powered by a 110hp Clerget 9Z engine when Harry Hawker got in its cockpit and, as he put it, 'bounced into the air' from Brooklands aerodrome on 26 December. The torque of the rotary engine, combined with the concentration of weight up front, endowed it with breathtaking manoeuvrability, but Hawker noted the sensitivity of the controls, which required a judicious hand, especially during take-off.

Two subsequent unserialled prototypes were designated the F 1/2, a naval prototype, and the F 1/3, which was flown with the 130hp Clerget 9B, 110hp Le Rhône 9J and the experimental Clerget LS (Long Stroke), later rechristened the 140hp Clerget 9Bf. It was allegedly when the latter was delivered to Martlesham Heath on 24 March 1917 that one of the RFC Testing Squadron's pilots said, 'Just to look at the beast gives me the hump at the thought of flying it'. That remark, recorded by RFC technical officer Sir Harry Tizard, along with the gun fairing's appearance, led to the sobriquet 'Camel', which like 'Pup' was never official, but nevertheless gained universal acceptance.

As the F 1 developed, tapered wings with a single, plank-shaped interplane strut were tried, but when the so-called F 1/1, powered by a 130hp Clerget 9B, was flown by the RFC Testing Squadron at Martlesham Heath in May 1917, the altered arrangement failed to yield the improved performance Sopwith had hoped for. One alteration that was adopted was a cutout in the upper wing centre section to alleviate the pilot's restricted view upward and forward – a significant weakness that would lead to larger

SOPWITH F 1 CAMEL

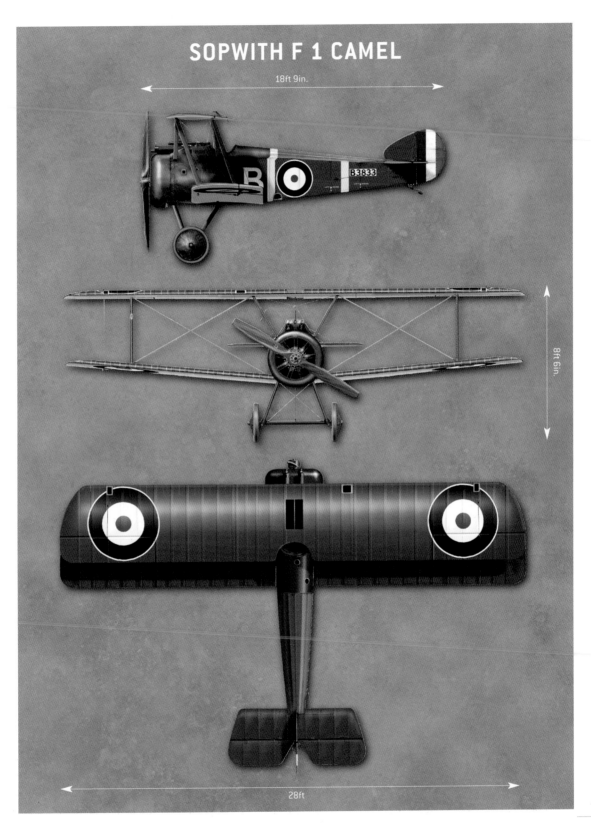

18ft 9in.

8ft 6in.

28ft

apertures being made on production Camels by pilots in the field. The prototype's one-piece upper wing was also replaced by one built in three sections for production aircraft.

May 1917 also saw the second naval prototype, N518, test flown at Martlesham Heath with a new 150hp AR 1 ('Admiralty Rotary No. 1'). This engine enjoyed better reliability than the Clerget thanks to its steel-lined aluminium cylinders, designed by RNAS engineering liaison officer Wilfred Owen Bentley. The engine gave such outstanding performance that it was put into production as the Bentley BR 1, which powered the first operational Camels, and became the best of their many powerplants.

Also developed from the F 1 were specialized naval variants. A twin-float seaplane failed to find favour, but more successful was the 2F 1, which featured shorter-span wings, a narrower track undercarriage, a hinged, folding tail for shipboard storage, slim steel tube cabane struts and a single Vickers gun, supplemented by an unsynchronized 0.303in. Lewis gun on a Foster-type mounting, firing above the upper wing.

Operating from warships and towed lighters, the 2F 1 Camel enjoyed a successful career of its own, its exploits including the first interception from an aircraft carrier – one of two bomb-armed floatplanes driven into the North Sea by two Camels from HMS *Furious* on 18 June 1918 – the bombing of Zeppelin airships L 54 and L 60 in their sheds at Tondern by *Furious'* Camels on 18 July and the airborne destruction of L 53 by a lighter-launched 2F 1 flown by Lt Stuart Culley on 10 August 1918.

Sopwith Triplane prototype N500 suffers a noseover. Australian ace Flt Lt Roderic Stanley Dallas of No. 1 Wing's 'A' Squadron used this machine to down a German two-seater on 1 July 1916, followed by an enemy fighter on 30 September. (Brian Kehew via Rod Filan)

In early June 1917, No. 4 Sqn RNAS began replacing its Pups. On the 4th, Flt Cdr Alexander M. Shook, patrolling in Camel N6347, attacked an enemy aeroplane 15 miles off Nieuport, which dived and escaped in a dense sea haze. Engaging 15 German aircraft between Nieuport and Ostende at 1900hrs the next day, Shook sent a scout crashing on the beach and drove a two-seater down out of control ten minutes later.

The first frontline Camel loss occurred on 13 June when American volunteer Flt Sub-Lt Langley F. W. Smith, who had eight victories to his credit flying Pups, was killed in N6362. Some witnesses said his Camel broke up while he was stunting above the German aerodrome at Neumünster.

The Camels of No. 4 Sqn RNAS, joined by those of 'Naval 3', chalked up several more successes in June and July. On 10 July, however, Flt Sub-Lt E. W. Busby was killed in action, and two days later 'Naval 4' was reminded of the new aeroplane's unforgiving nature when Canadian Flt Sub-Lt Sydney E. Ellis, who had claimed two victories in Pups and three in the Camel, fatally spun into the ground. Notwithstanding that cautionary mishap, it had been a satisfactory first month for the touchy, but nimble, debutante.

Canadian-born Flt Cdr Alexander M. Shook (left) of No. 4 Sqn RNAS, who drew first blood for the Camel on 5 June 1917, poses with Triplane and Camel ace Flt Cdr Charles D. Booker of No. 8 Sqn RNAS. (Stuart Leslie/Jack Bruce Collection)

FOKKER Dr I

Whilst the first Camels were being delivered to the front, the Sopwith Triplane had been making its presence felt amid the Allied aerial debacle known as 'Bloody April', taking a noticeable toll of German aircraft. Although Manfred von Richthofen managed to vanquish a Triplane for his 52nd victory on 29 April, killing Canadian Flt Sub-Lt Albert E. Cuzner of No. 8 Sqn RNAS, the scout's performance left enough of an impression for the influential Baron to join the clamour for a new fighter to counter it.

The Inspektion der Fliegertruppen, or Idflieg, responded in much the same way as it had done when the Nieuport 11 *Bébé* arrived on the scene in 1916. Some German manufacturers simply copied the French fighter, while others produced original designs. In the latter camp were Albatros with its D III sesquiplane and Pfalz with its D III biplane cellule with a much-reduced lower wing area. In June 1917, Idflieg issued a general request for copies of the triplane formula.

At that time Anthony Fokker, whose fortunes had been in decline due to his failure to keep pace with the new Albatros fighters, had been developing a series of prototype scouts based on a box spar wing structure pioneered by Swedish-born engineer Villehad Forssman. Fokker was also familiar with the all-metal cantilever wing structures developed by Dr Hugo Junkers, the strength of which the latter had proven when his J I monoplane took to the air on 12 December 1915. Fokker, however, decided that Forssman's wooden structure offered a lighter-weight airframe that would make the most of the limited power that engines of the time could then provide.

The first of Fokker's experimental *Verspannungslos* ('without external bracing') designs – the V 1 and V 2 – were sesquiplanes with plywood-covered wings and fuselages, powered by air-cooled rotary and water-cooled inline engines, respectively. Tested in early 1917, they showed great potential months prior to the issuing of Idflieg's triplane requirement in June of that year.

Although Fokker was among the German designers least interested in building a triplane fighter at that point in the war, he was hardly one to pass up an opportunity to regain his prominence in the industry. Fokker therefore took the fuselage of a V 3 – a rotary-engined biplane fighter that he had been building for the Austro-Hungarian air service – and reconfigured it as the V 4 triplane. To save weight, the latter used a canvas, rather than plywood, covering over a steel tube fuselage frame and plywood box spar wing structure.

The prototype originally featured simple non-balanced elevators and ailerons and no interplane struts on the wings, but as the latter were slightly lengthened, they required a set of I-shaped interplane struts and balanced control surfaces. The V 4 was powered by a captured 110hp Le Rhône engine, but its successor was fitted with an Oberursel Ur II – the German-built copy of the French rotary.

While the improved V 4 version (later redesignated V 5) was undergoing testing in late June, Fokker was busy building the V 6. This variant featured a 160hp Mercedes water-cooled inline engine, but it proved to be heavy, slow and sluggish when compared to its rotary counterpart. The V 4/5, however, had impressed its pilots and Idflieg favourably enough for Fokker to begin work on three pre-production F Is,

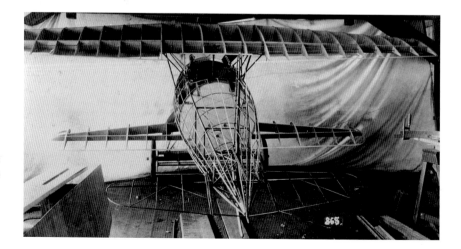

A stripped-down V 1 displays the innovative wooden box cantilever wing structure that Anthony Fokker adopted because it was lighter than Dr Hugo Junkers' all-metal configuration – as well as the sesquiplane configuration he had had in mind before the Idflieg insisted upon a triplane layout. (Museum of Flight Peter Bowers Collection)

the 'F' designator merely being the lowest letter in the alphabet not used by the Luftstreitskräfte thus far.

On 26 July 1917, von Richthofen – a day after returning to JG I's aerodrome at Marcke following his recovery from a head wound that he had suffered 20 days earlier – announced to his officers that they were soon to be re-equipped with 'new Fokker triplanes, which climb like apes and are as manoeuvrable as the devil'. The first pre-production machine, F I 101/17, was tested to destruction on 11 August, but on the 28th the remaining two F Is arrived at Marcke. F I 102/17 went to von Richthofen, whose score then stood at 59. The other, 103/17, was issued to Jasta 10's commander, Ltn Werner Voss, a 38-victory ace who was engaged in an amicable, but nonetheless earnest, rivalry with his Geschwaderkommandeur.

Their friendship notwithstanding, the two aces differed considerably in fighting style and temperament. Although von Richthofen was not as natural a pilot as Voss, he was a superb tactician with murderously efficient hunting instincts and, as testified by his men, uncanny vision. Voss, highly-strung and impulsive, was master of any aeroplane he flew, and a deadly shot.

Von Richthofen regarded the F I, with its advanced structure, agility and rate-of-climb, as the hoped-for panacea to the structurally unreliable Albatros D V and relatively sluggish Pfalz D III. Voss, equally disillusioned with both machines, had already test flown the V 4, and upon the F I's arrival on 28 August, immediately embraced it as a fighter just made for a man of his talents.

The first frontline test came on the morning of 1 September, as von Richthofen reported:

Flying the triplane for the first time in combat, I and four gentlemen of Staffel 11 attacked a very courageously flown British artillery-spotting aircraft. I approached until it was 50 metres below me and fired 20 shots, whereupon the adversary went down out of control and crashed on this side near Zonnebeke.

OPPOSITE

Fokker Dr I 477/17 of
Rittm Manfred Freiherr von
Richthofen, Jasta 11, based
at Léchelle on 7 April 1918.
Von Richthofen is credited
with the destruction of eight
Camels, claiming two apiece
in Dr Is 127/17, 152/17,
425/17 and 477/17. The last,
which from his description
was finished in an identical
manner to the first two
(leaving only 425/17
confirmed as being all-red),
figured in nine of his victories,
including Camels downed on
25 March and 7 April 1918.
477/17 is shown here after
having its crosses altered
to the new straight form
ordered, but not always
immediately implemented,
after 17 March 1918.

Anthony Fokker prepares for
take-off in the pre-production
F I 102/17, while Rittm von
Richthofen looks on. This
view shows the F I's more
rounded horizontal stabilizer
compared to the example
fitted to the production Dr I.

Apparently the adversary had taken me for a British triplane, as the observer stood up in his machine without making a move to attack me with his machine gun.

The Baron's 60th victim was RE 8 B782 of No. 6 Sqn RFC. The wounded pilot, Lt J. B. C. Madge, was taken prisoner, and his observer, 2Lt Walter Kember, was killed.

Two days later, Jasta 11's morning patrol attacked Pups from No. 46 Sqn RFC over Menin, five kilometres from Marcke. Pup pilot Lt Arthur Stanley Gould Lee described the action in a letter whose text he must have altered in the process of compiling it into his autobiography, *No Parachute*, since both F Is wore streaky greenish camouflage with light blue undersurfaces, with no overpainted colours at the time:

The first patrol ran quickly into trouble when five of 'A' Flight met von Richthofen's Circus and had a hectic scrap. The Pups were completely outclassed by the D Vs, and most of their share of the fighting consisted of trying to avoid being riddled. Mac (2Lt K . W. McDonald) and (2Lt Algernon F.) Bird were seen to go down in Hunland. (Lt Richard) Asher might have reached the Lines. The two chaps who got away, badly shot about, said that one of the Huns was flying a triplane, coloured red. It must be a captured naval Tripe, I suppose.

McDonald was shot down and killed for Ltn Eberhardt Mohnicke's sixth victory. Von Richthofen drove the other Pup down south of Bousbecque, although not without a fight, as he reported;

I was absolutely convinced that in front of me I had a very skillful pilot, who even at 50 metres altitude did not give up, continued to fire and, even when flattening out (before landing), fired at an infantry column and then deliberately steered his machine into a tree. The Fokker F I 102/17 is absolutely superior to the British Sopwith.

FOKKER Dr I

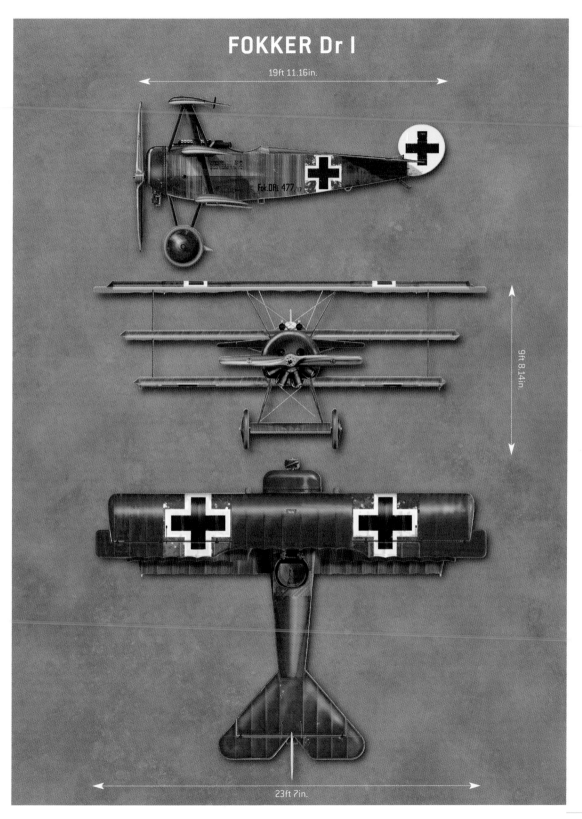

19ft 11.16in.

9ft 8.14in.

23ft 7in.

Both von Richthofen and Anthony Fokker, who was visiting Marcke seeking an opportunity to promote his new fighter, hastened to the crash site. There, Fokker photographed von Richthofen beside his captive, who, in spite of his misfortune, looked quite pleased to have done his duty as best the circumstances allowed, and to have survived his run-in with the Red Baron. While Fokker was recording F I 102/17 and its famous pilot for posterity on his ciné camera, at 0955hrs Voss downed a Camel, killing Lt A. T. Heywood of No. 45 Sqn RFC, north of Houthem.

After that day's success, von Richthofen went on three weeks' leave, placing Ltn Kurt von Döring in acting command of JG I and his triplane in the care of Ltn Kurt Wolff. The latter assumed command of Jasta 11 on 11 September, and was promoted to oberleutnant the next day. Wolff, who had 33 victories to his credit, was depressed at having not scored since 7 July, and was keen to regain his winning streak in the new triplane.

Voss may have been flying F I 103/17 on 3 September, in which case he had scored the first Fokker triplane victory over a Camel. He was certainly flying it on the 5th, when he downed a Pup whose pilot, 2Lt Charles W. Odell of No. 46 Sqn RFC, was fortunate enough to land in Allied lines unhurt.

'They were patrolling northeast of Ypres when Odell, who had seen a triplane coming down from behind, but taken no notice, thinking it was a Nautical, was amazed to find it firing at him', Arthur Gould Lee wrote. 'He turned, assuming the RNAS pilot had gone off his rocker, then saw the black crosses. The others turned too, and a brisk little scrap followed, the Hun being joined by a D V. The triplane, which was painted red, had a tremendous performance, and when he decided he'd had enough he lifted up above everybody like a rocket. He was a pretty hot pilot, for he holed most of the Pups, but nobody could get a bead on him.'

Again, Lee referred, perhaps retrospectively, to a colour that neither F I had, but the German's flying style is clearly that of Voss, who also downed a Caudron G 6 of French *escadrille* C53 in flames that day and destroyed an FE 2d of No. 20 Sqn RFC 24 hours later.

Voss was in his triplane when he destroyed two Camels between 1750hrs and 1755hrs on 10 September, killing 2Lts A. J. S. Sisley and O. C. Pearson of No. 70 Sqn RFC, and claimed a SPAD VII of Spa 37 20 minutes later. He downed two more Camels the next day, the pilot of one, six-victory ace Lt Oliver L. McMaking of No. 45 Sqn RFC, being killed east of St Julien. Voss in turn was credited to McMaking's squadronmate Capt Norman MacMillan, as not one but two triplanes were driven down by him 'out of control' east of Langemarck – the sixth and seventh of an eventual nine victories.

Flt Sub-Lt Norman M. Macgregor at No. 10 Sqn RNAS' aerodrome at Droglandt. Though not the first to claim a Fokker triplane, on 15 September he became the first Camel pilot to actually destroy one, killing Oblt Kurt Wolff of Jasta 11 in F I 102/17. (Mike Westrop)

In fact, through the violent manoeuvres that caused the misconception among his enemies (MacMillan believed there were three triplanes involved in the fight!), Voss emerged unscathed, having raised his tally by nine in about as many days. He now had 47 victories to his credit.

On 15 September, Wolff led a patrol, only to become separated from his Albatrosen. At about 1630hrs, however, Jasta 11 dived on a four-Camel flight from No. 10 Sqn RNAS over Moorslede, and Wolff joined in. Although attacked from above, the British managed to evade the Germans' fire and a general engagement ensued, during which Flt Sub-Lt Norman M. Macgregor, credited with four previous victories while in No. 6 Sqn RNAS, fired into the triplane at 25yds' distance, saw it fall in a steep dive and claimed it as 'out of control'.

All too often, 'out of control' merely signified a clever job of evasion by the enemy, but this time the Camel had indeed drawn first blood against its classic counterpart – Wolff's body was found in the wreckage of F I 102/17 near Nachtigal, north of Werwicq.

At 0930hrs on 23 September, Voss destroyed a de Havilland DH 4 of No. 57 Sqn RFC south of Roulers. His score now stood at 48, but a squadronmate, Ltn Aloys Heldmann, noticed the toll the past month's activity was taking on him. 'He was on edge. He had the nervous instability of a cat. I think it would be fair to say that he was flying on his nerves. And such a situation could have but one end'.

Joining his brothers Otto and Max for lunch, Werner Voss discussed plans for his upcoming leave. At 1800hrs he led five other fighters on the day's last patrol, but when he spotted a patrol of SE 5as from No. 60 Sqn RFC over Poelkapelle, Voss, keen to raise his score to an even 50 before departing Jasta 10, dove on the British scouts. He was in turn jumped by the SE 5as of 'B' Flight No. 56 Sqn RFC.

The epic ten-minute dogfight that followed was documented by the testimonies of some of Britain's most seasoned fighter pilots, and they were all awed by the virtuosity of Voss, his triplane, and by the damage they inflicted. Of No. 60 Sqn's flight, Capt Harold A. Hamersley came down with his engine shot up and Capt Robert L Chidlaw-Roberts returned with his rudder bar shot through, while in 'Fighting 56', Lt Keith K. Muspratt retired with a bullet in his radiator and 2Lt Verschoyle P. Cronyn limped home with his wings so badly riddled he spent that night in a 'sweaty funk', unable to sleep.

The remains of Fokker F I 102/17 near Nachtigal after it was shot down by Camel pilot Flt Sub-Lt N. M. Macgregor on 15 September 1917. (Paul Mirich via Rod Filan)

Ltn Werner Voss with Fokker F I 103/17 – a pairing of man and machine that put the seal of approval on the triplane, but which ultimately cost Voss his life. (Greg VanWyngarden)

That left Voss and an Albatros D V that came to his aid to tackle such No. 56 Sqn paladins as James T. B. McCudden, Arthur P. F. Rhys Davids, Reginald T. C. Hoidge, Richard A. Maybery and 'C' Flight's leader, Capt Geoffrey Hilton Bowman. Several of them marvelled at the manoeuvres through which Voss put his machine, several others noting what Bowman reported:

> I put my nose down to give him a burst and opened fire, perhaps too soon. To my amazement he kicked on full rudder, without bank, pulled his nose up slightly, gave me a burst while he was skidding sideways and then kicked on opposite rudder before the results of this amazing stunt appeared to have any effect on the controllability of his machine.

Eventually Rhys Davids drove down the Albatros, whose pilot, Ltn Karl Menckhoff of Jasta 3, survived, and then he shot down 103/17 at Plum Farm, 700 metres north of Frezenburg, where an ongoing battle compelled the first soldiers on the scene to hastily bury Voss' body near the crash site. Still, the German ace's last fight made him and his triplane the talk of No. 56 Sqn that night. The two F Is' overall performance that month – at least six victories by Voss, including four Camels, and two victories by von Richthofen – put the seal of approval on Fokker's new fighter.

The production model, redesignated Dr I (for *Dreidecker*, or triplane) differed from the F I by having a modified cowling, a straight rather than slightly curved leading edge to the horizontal stabilizer and the attachment of two wooden skids at the lower end of the interplane struts to protect the undersides of the wings in case of ground loops. While the F Is and early Dr Is had ailerons of different square metrage to compensate for the engine torque, those of later Dr Is had identical ailerons of increased area.

In the month following Voss' death, JG I's pilots were assigned a few Fokker D V fighter trainers to familiarize them with the idiosyncrasies of rotary engines. When von Richthofen returned to Marcke on 23 October, Jasta 11 got 17 of the much-anticipated Dr Is.

The Circus' elation with the new machines would be short-lived. On 29 October, a German pilot mistook Vzfw Josef Lautenschlager's Dr I 113/17 for a Sopwith Triplane and sent him crashing to his death north of Houthulst Forest. The next day, both Lothar and Manfred von Richthofen had to force-land their malfunctioning Dr Is. A more alarming mishap occurred elsewhere that day when Ltn Heinrich Gontermann, commander of Jasta 15 and a 39-victory ace, test flew his newly delivered Dr I 115/17 over La Neuville aerodrome, only to see the ribs break away from the aircraft's upper wing spar, resulting in a crash from which he succumbed to his injuries that evening.

Before anyone could regard Gontermann's as an exceptional case, on 31 October, von Richthofen noticed Ltn Günther Pastor of Jasta 11 gliding down to land when his Dr I (121/17) dropped its port wing and crashed. There was no sign of corrective measures being made or succeeding before the triplane hit the ground, killing Pastor.

On 2 November, an alarmed Idflieg grounded all Dr Is and a crash commission examined the triplane's wing in the hope of pinpointing the cause. Its findings centred not on the box spar structure, which was inherently sound, but the ribs and aileron attachment points behind it, neither of which were attached to the box spar.

At low angles of attack – as in a dive – the forces of lift move aft on a wing, which would cause the Dr I's ribs to flex. Similar flexing occurred on the ailerons, which were more pronounced on the V 4, with increased span, and its production derivatives. While the F Is had been able to handle those stresses, the Dr Is had not because their unvarnished wing interiors had absorbed moisture, weakening the glue – already thinned as an economic measure – that helped hold them together.

The committee's conclusion was that Fokker needed to improve his quality control, among other things using cold-water glue of more robust consistency, transverse nailing to reinforce the glue and a more thorough application of varnish over the wing structure before applying the fabric covering. The left aileron's aerodynamic balance was reduced, but a decrease of inboard taper increased the overall aileron area, reducing stress and increasing the roll rate to the right (a feature that could come in particularly handy against Camels). The newer aileron became standard on both sides of the upper wings fitted by Fokker to later production Dr Is.

Although the improved workmanship did much to improve the Dr I's safety, von Richthofen, cognizant of winter weather conditions in Flanders, demanded wooden sheds for JG I's triplanes. Where such structures might be impracticable, as during the rapid advances in April 1918, he settled for hangar tents to provide his fighters with at least a measure of shelter.

Deliveries resumed in late December, and in January 1918 Jasta 11 re-equipped with Dr Is featuring the modified wings, soon to be joined by Jasta 6. The Fokker triplane was now ready to make its much-delayed debut in force.

TECHNICAL
SPECIFICATIONS

SOPWITH CAMEL

The Sopwith Camel's fabric-covered wire-braced wooden structure was well-established long before it was conceived, and was as straightforward as its development. Besides the parent Sopwith Aviation Co. Ltd, Boulton & Paul Ltd, British Caudron Co. Ltd, Hooper & Co. Ltd, March, Jones & Cribb Ltd, Portholme Aerodrome Ltd and Ruston, Proctor & Co. Ltd were contracted to produce airframes to satisfy orders that totalled 5,695 by the end of the war. In contrast, just 320 serial numbers have been identified for Fokker Dr Is built by May 1918, when production ceased in favour of the D VII.

The key to the Camel's performance was the concentration of weight and power in a compact space, and it used a number of engine types, experimental and operational. By the end of 1917, a total of 3,450 Camels had been ordered and 1,325 delivered to the services. During that time 1,546 Clerget and 540 Le Rhône engines passed inspection for use, an additional 875 Clergets and 1,314 Le Rhônes of French manufacture had also arrived and the first 269 Bentley BR 1s had been built.

In July 1917, both the 140hp Clerget 9Bf and 150hp Bentley BR 1 engines were tested with different compression ratios in an attempt to wring more output from them. Testing at Martlesham led to a Clerget with a higher ratio of 5.29 to 1 that became standard for Camels thereafter. Of five such variations tested on the BR 1, the best results came from installing larger induction pipes with a 2mm hole bored into the top casing of each. The result was a compression ratio of 5.7 to 1, and 11 more horsepower.

On 31 October 1918, the RAF had 385 BR 1-powered Camels, 1,342 powered by Clergets and 821 with Le Rhône or 150hp Gnome Monosoupape engines. The latter, first tested on a Camel at Martlesham in December 1917, featured dual

PERFORMANCE FIGURES OF CAMEL ENGINES

Aircraft	F 1/1		B2512		F 1/3		B3829		N518	
Engine	130hp		130hp		140hp		110hp		150hp	
	Clerget		Clerget		Clerget 9Bf		Le Rhône		BR 1	
Weight (lb)										
Empty	950		962		–		–		977	
Loaded	1,482		1,482		1,452		1,422		1,508	
Maximum speed (mph)										
At 6,500ft	–		108		–		–		116.5	
At 10,000ft	112.5		104.5		–		108.5		111	
At 15,000ft	106		97.5		113.5		111.5		103	
Climb to	min	sec	min	sec	min	sec	min	sec	min	sec
6,500ft	6	00	6	40	5	00	5	10	5	30
10,000ft	10	35	11	45	8	30	9	10	9	50
15,000ft	21	5	23	15	15	45	16	50	20	00
Service ceiling (ft)										
	19,000		18,500		24,000		24,000		18,500	
Endurance (hours)										
	2¾		–		–		–		2½	

A view of a Sopwith Camel cockpit. The amount, and placement, of instrumentation was not uniform, and the presence of a 'blip switch' on the control column depended on whether the aeroplane had a Le Rhône or Gnome engine. Pilots of Bentley BR 1-powered Camels operated a throttle.
(Philip Jarrett)

SOPWITH F 1 CAMEL COCKPIT

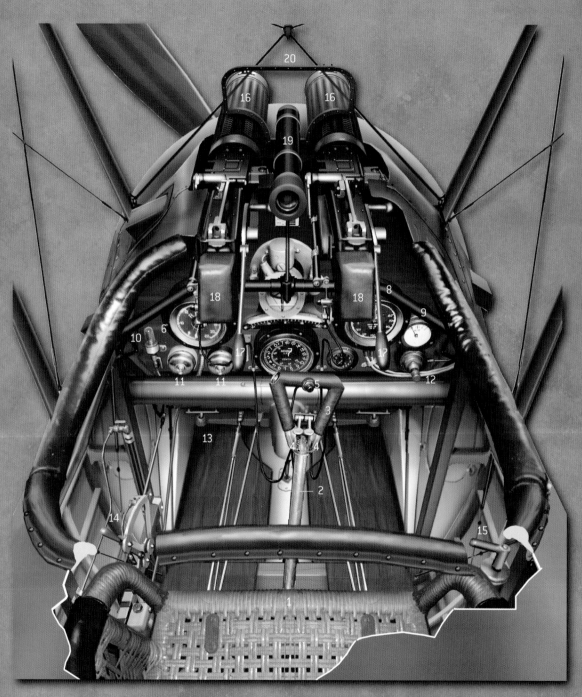

1. Seat
2. Control column
3. Spade grip
4. Machine gun buttons
5. Blip switch
6. Tachometer
7. Altimeter
8. Airspeed indicator
9. Air pressure gauge
10. Pulsator
11. Magnetic switch
12. Throttle (BR 1 Camel)
13. Rudder bar
14. Petrol fine-adjustment lever
15. Fuel pressurization hand pump
16. 0.303-in. Vickers machine guns
17. Cocking levers
18. Gun padding
19. Aldis gunsight
20. Windscreen

Aircraft	B3835		B3811		USAS Camel		F6394	
Engine	150hp		100hp		150hp		170hp	
	BR 1		Gnome		Gnome		Le Rhône	
Weight (lb)								
Empty	–		882		–		1,048	
Loaded	1,470		1,387		1,523		1,567	
Maximum speed (mph)								
At 6,500ft	–		–		–		–	
At 10,000ft	121		110.5		117.5		113	
At 15,000ft	114.5		102.5		107		108.5	
Climb to	min	sec	min	sec	min	sec	min	sec
6,500ft	4	35	6	50	5	50	5	30
10,000ft	8	20	11	50	10	20	9	35
15,000ft	15	55	23	15	19	40	17	30
Service ceiling (ft)								
	22,000		18,500		21,500		21,500	
Endurance (hours)								
	2½		2¾		2¼		–	

ignition, with two spark plugs per cylinder, and a multi-position ignition switch that enabled it to run on nine, seven, five, three or one cylinder. Although the Gnome's performance figures compared well with the BR 1's, it was not adopted for British use. When the United States Army Air Service (USAS) bought a consignment of Camels, it also bought a number of Gnomes for them, but Boulton & Paul's attempt to install the engines on its Camel airframes was brief and unsuccessful. Performance figures for some of the Camel engine installations are listed in the accompanying tables.

The F 1 Camel had a wingspan of 28ft, a chord of 4ft 6in. and a wing area of 231 sq. ft. The four ailerons had an area of 9 sq. ft each, the tailplane's was 14 sq. ft, the elevators 10.5 sq. ft, the vertical stablilizer 3 sq. ft and the rudder 4.9 sq. ft. The 5ft wing gap at the fuselage diminished at the wingtips due to the 5-degree dihedral of the lower wing compared with none for the upper.

The Camel's overall length varied with its engine – 18ft 9in. with the Clerget; 18ft 8in. with the 110hp Le Rhône; 18ft 6in. with the BR 1 or 150hp Gnome Monosoupape; and 19ft with the 100hp Monosoupape or 170hp Le Rhône.

Synchronization for the F 1's twin 0.303in. Vickers machine guns also varied with the engine. Those powered by the 100hp Le Rhône used a Constantinesco C C synchronizing mechanism, while those fitted with the 130hp Clerget used Kauper No. 3 interruptor gear. Aldis ring and bead sights were standard on all Camels, but individual pilots in the frontline often replaced them with a variety of sights of their own choosing.

In addition to its machine guns, the Camel could carry four 20lb Cooper bombs in racks under the fuselage, making it a more versatile warplane than the Fokker

Dr I. Besides trench strafing, on 19 July 1918, 2F 1 naval Camels made history when six of them took off from the aircraft carrier *Furious* and bombed the German airship sheds at Tondern, burning Zeppelins L 54 and L 60 in the first bombing raid ever launched from a carrier deck.

To combat the threat of Gotha and Zeppelin-Staaken night bombing attacks on British cities, Camel-equipped Home Defence squadrons developed a variant called the Sopwith Comic, which replaced the Vickers with twin Lewis guns firing over the upper wing on a double Foster mounting, with the cockpit set farther back on the fuselage and the pilot furnished with Hutton or Neame illuminated sights. This arrangement was devised so that the gun flashes would not be directly in front of the pilot, ruining his night vision.

FOKKER Dr I

While the British were experimenting to wring more performance from the Camel's engines, the principal development work on the Fokker Dr I in early 1918 was to provide it with a halfway dependable powerplant. While the triplane was a match for the Camel, other Allied aircraft, such as the SE 5a, SPAD, Bristol Fighter or de Havilland DH 4, could easily outrun the German fighter if their pilots chose to, especially at higher altitudes.

Although the Dr I's maximum speed was originally cited as 102.5mph at 13,120ft, careful calculations made during German test flights at Rechlin aerodrome in April 1918 yielded statistics of 97mph at 9,200ft and only 86mph at 13,800ft. Amid the *Kaiserschlacht*, Manfred von Richthofen reportedly remarked that JG I could have downed six times as many opponents as it did were it not for the Dr I's inability to keep up with them.

The principal Fokker triplane engine was the Oberursel Ur II, which was a copy of the French 110hp Le Rhône. At least 12 Dr Is are known to have used the 110hp Goebel Goe II seven-cylinder rotary engine, and on 30 October 1917, Dr I 108/17 was test flown with a 160hp Goe III, which yielded better performance. On 14 December 1917, Dr I 417/17, with a lengthened fuselage, was test flown with a Goe III under a cowling of increased diameter. It is possible that Dr I 201/17 was also test flown with a 178hp Goe IIIa, but in spite of the favourable results, there is no evidence that Goebel-engined Dr Is saw use except by home defence units.

Another Dr I airframe was tested with the 160hp Siemens und Halske Sh III 11-cylinder rotary-radial engine, which rotated in an opposite direction to the airscrew. As with Siemens-Schuckert Werke's own D III fighter, the engine gave the Fokker a spectacular rate-of-climb and vastly improved service ceiling. However, it was still unreliable, its torque made the aeroplane tricky to handle and the tall undercarriage required to compensate for the larger two- and four-bladed propellers used with the Sh III meant that the triplane was now a challenge to land as well.

Another attempt to improve the Ur II's performance was the installation of an experimental Schwade gear-driven compressor. This early form of supercharger proved to be successful, but it was never used operationally on Dr Is. The fact that it did

Captured intact on 13 January 1918, Ltn Eberhardt Stapenhorst's Fokker Dr I 144/17 was stripped down for a thorough evaluation – the resulting photographs providing posterity with some useful interior views. (Museum of Flight Peter Bowers Collection)

work on a rotary engine, however, indicated that it probably would have been used on the Fokker E V/D VIII parasol monoplane fighter had the war lasted longer.

Yet another experimental engine installation, made at Fokker's request, was the 145hp Oberursel 11-cylinder Ur III. Produced in December 1917, it was tested on Dr I 469/17.

Undermining the effectiveness of all of Germany's rotary engines was their need for castor oil, readily available to the Allies but not to the Germans, who strove to develop a synthetic substitute. It was probably in the course of testing such ersatz lubricants that Dr Is 485/17, 527/17 and 562/17 were fitted with captured 130hp Clerget engines, and 100/18 was test-flown with a captured 160hp Gnome Monosoupape, all in April 1918. Dr I 195/17 was experimentally fitted with what was described as a 'Rhenania Le Rhône' – probably a Ur II licence-built by the Rhenania Motorenfabrik AG in Mannheim (Rhemag), which was also contracted to produce the Siemens und Halske Sh III. Performance figures for some of the Dr I engine installations are listed in the accompanying table.

For all the efforts put into it, the Dr I never acquired an engine of comparable reliability to the Camel's, which handicapped its effectiveness during the spring of 1918 and practically drove it from the skies as the summer taxed its synthetic lubricants beyond their limits. By June, however, the Fokker D VII, a biplane that reverted to the more proven water-cooled Mercedes and BMW engines, and which offered superior overall performance, was arriving in quantity to render the matter moot. At that point, the Fokker triplane went from being the best German fighter over the Western Front to a hand-me-down second-best for units awaiting their D VIIs.

Engine	110hp		145hp		160hp		160hp	
	Le Rhône		Oberursel Ur III		Goebel Goe III		Sh III	
Weight (lb)								
Empty	894		948		970		1,082	
Loaded	1,290		1,378		1,400		1,512	
Maximum speed (mph)								
Unspecified	–		115		118		120	
altitude								
At 13,120ft	102.5		–		–		–	
Climb to	min	sec	min	sec	min	sec	min	sec
6,560ft	6	5	4	20	4	0	–	–
9,840ft	10	5	7	5	7	0	–	–
13,120ft	15	15	10	50	10	0	–	–
16,400ft	23	50	15	30	14	0	–	–
Service ceiling (ft)								
	20,000		24,280		27,230		–	
Endurance (hours)								
	1 ½		–		–		–	

FOKKER Dr I COCKPIT

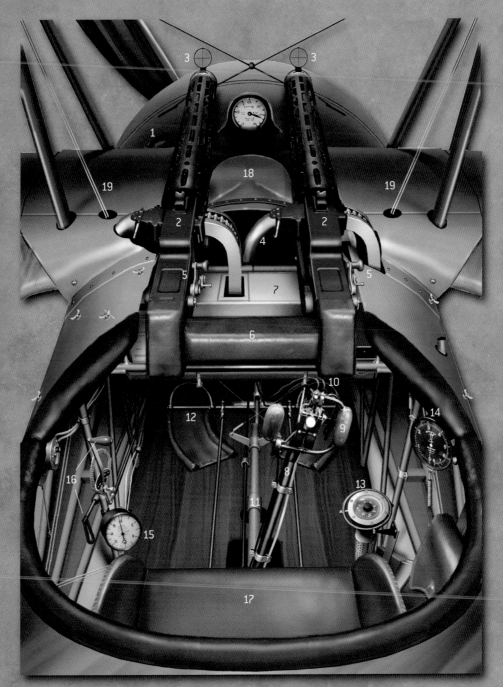

1. Fuel filler cap
2. 7.92mm LMG 08/15 machine guns
3. Ring and bead sights
4. Ammunition chutes
5. Cocking levers
6. Gun padding
7. Ammunition boxes
8. Control column
9. Control column-mounted secondary throttle control
10. Machine gun buttons
11. Control column mounting shaft
12. Rudder control bar
13. Compass
14. Altimeter
15. Airspeed indicator
16. Engine throttle and fuel cock controls
17. Aluminium seat (with plywood base and leather covering)
18. Windscreen
19. Aileron control cables

A look inside the cockpit of Dr I 581/17, showing the spartan instrument arrangement compared to the Camel's. As with the Camel, the Fokker's machine gun butts were well padded in case of a noseover. (Alex Imrie)

Spans on the Dr I were 23ft 7.08in. for the upper wing, 20ft 5.08in. for the middle and 18ft 9.4in. for the lower wing. The gap between upper and middle wings was 2ft 10.45in. and 2ft 9.66in. between middle and lower wings. The area of the upper wing came to 81.59 sq. ft, compared to 54.25 sq. ft for the middle, 52.31 sq. ft for the lower wing and an additional 12.7 sq. ft for the undercarriage airfoil, for a grand total of 200.85 sq. ft. Each of the the two ailerons had an area of 0.8 sq. ft, while the tailplane and elevators had a total of 29 sq. ft and the rudder 7.1 sq. ft. Dihedral was nil on all three wings.

In spite of a rather generous wheel track of 5ft 5.75in., the lateral instability of the Dr I's configuration, combined with poor downward visibility from the cockpit, made it as tricky to land as the Camel. Cutouts in the after part of the middle wings gave the pilot an improved downward view during his critical landing run. If it was allowed to stall at low height, the left wing tended to drop first.

Length for the Le Rhône and Oberursel powered Dr Is was 19ft 11.16in., and 20ft 11.96in. for the Goebel-engined machines. Overall height came to 9ft 8.14in. Stagger also varied – 9.05in. between upper and middle wings, and 8.86in. between middle and lower wings. The maximum tailspan was 8ft 7.15in. The Axial propeller on operational Dr Is had a diameter of 8ft 7.15in. Armament was limited to two fixed 7.92mm LMG 08/15s with 1,000 rounds of ammunition, synchronized using Fokker's *Zentralsteurung* interruptor gear.

As with the Camel, the Dr I's inherent instability necessitated its pilot to fly it all the time. Ltn Rudolf Stark, a Pfalz D IIIa ace who got to fly hand-me-down Dr Is for a time in Royal Bavarian Jagdstaffel 34, wrote of his first impression:

Flying these new machines is at first naturally very unfamiliar. Light and sensitive, they follow the slightest movement of the controls. They climb like a lift, and in the twinkling of an eye are several hundred metres high. One can turn on a spot like a top. The operation of the rotary engine has to be learned first though, and in the beginning created some difficulties.

So, adding up all the performance statistics, how did the Camel and Fokker Dr I stack up in a theoretical one-on-one match between pilots of equal skill? When it came to manoeuvrability, the Dr I held a slight edge, partly because its layout was not quite as extreme as the Camel's, and partially because of its shorter wingspan, the overall greater lift the three wings and axle fairing afforded it and its balanced ailerons. Most telling was the fact that German pilots were advised to escape an attacking Camel using a right-hand turn – supposedly the Camel's forte, yet one that the Dr I could perform in a shorter radius that would eventually bring it onto the Camel's tail.

Ltn Walter Göttsch's Dr I 202/17 of Jasta 19 displays one dramatic consequence of engine overheating due to premature breakdown of the castor oil substitute devised by the Germans for their rotary engines – a problem that became worse in the summer months. (Alex Imrie)

Equally significant was the absence of German references to the Dr I having the Camel's vicious handling quirks, Ltn Heinz Graf von Gluszewski-Kwilicki of Jasta 4 going so far as to call the Fokker triplane 'The smoothest lovely ship I could fly after the Pfalz and Albatros'.

Being rotary-engined aircraft imposed speed limitations on both Camel and Dr I, further exacerbated by the drag produced by the latter's thick wings and the Camel's profusion of external bracing struts and wires. Still, even the slowest Camel had a slight edge in speed over the triplane, even when the latter's engine was working at full efficiency. Climb rates were roughly comparable, the Camel's being marginally slower or faster, again depending on its engine. The Camel's biplane wing layout offered better pilot visibility overall, even though the upper wing handicapped the view forward and above, leading many Camel pilots to cut away fabric from the upper centre section.

THE STRATEGIC SITUATION

The summer and autumn of 1917 had seen a series of Allied offensives in the Flanders, Champagne and Verdun regions peter out with little strategic gain for the exorbitant casualties they produced. The end of the year, on the other hand, had given the Central Powers reason for hope. The rout of the Italian army at Caporetto in October 1917 and the Russian Revolution, soon to be followed by Bolshevik capitulation in the Treaty of Brest-Litovsk on 3 March 1918, freed up multitudes of German soldiers for service on the Western Front.

More ominous news for Germany came from the Middle East, where the British were advancing steadily in Palestine and Mesopotamia, and from the United States, which had declared war on Germany on 6 April 1917 and was mobilizing its vast resources to ship an American Expeditionary Force (AEF) to France. To German strategic planners Paul von Hindenburg and Erich Ludendorff, the odds of mounting a victorious offensive, followed by a favourable peace with the Western Allies, were the highest they could ever hope for, but time was of the essence before the Americans arrived in full force.

For the breakthrough offensive, dubbed *Kaiserschlacht*, the Germans massed their aerial as well as ground assets, with three Jagdgeschwader (JG), each permanently formed around four Jastas by mid-February 1918, to augment more flexible *Jagdgruppen* fighter groups in establishing local air superiority over three different army groupings. JG I, assigned to II Armee, moved from its winter quarters at Avenses-le-Sec and Lieu-St-Armand on 20 March to re-establish itself at Awoingt, 5 kilometres south of Cambrai. Thinking ahead, von Richthofen had already chosen Léchelle, ten kilometres south-east of Bapaume, as his next base.

JG II, formed on 2 February 1918 with Jastas 12, 13, 15 and 19, initially had its headquarters at Toulis, but after the death of the Geschwaderführer, Hptm Adolf Ritter von Tutschek, on 15 March, the unit came under the command of Hptm Rudolf Berthold and, four days later, the wing moved to Guise to support the XVIII Armee.

Also formed on 2 February, JG III, commanded by Oblt Bruno Loerzer and consisting of Jastas Boelcke, 26, 27 and 36, took up its initial jumping-off point at Erchin, 10 kilometres south-east of Douai, to support the XVII Armee.

Although the Fokker Dr I was regarded by those who flew it as being the best overall fighter then in German service, von Richthofen and Berthold were already aware of limitations that even the modified triplanes could not overcome. The aircraft was slower than most of its contemporaries, and the Dr I's rotary engine – never a German strong suit – was chronically unreliable. The Geschwaderführer were also aware of at least two newer, extremely promising fighters in the offing. These were the Siemens-Schuckert Werke's SSW D III, with a 160hp Siemens und Halske Sh III 11-cylinder rotary-radial engine, and the Fokker D VII, a biplane variation on the Dr I theme, which had performed well with a 160hp Mercedes inline engine and even better with a 185hp BMW.

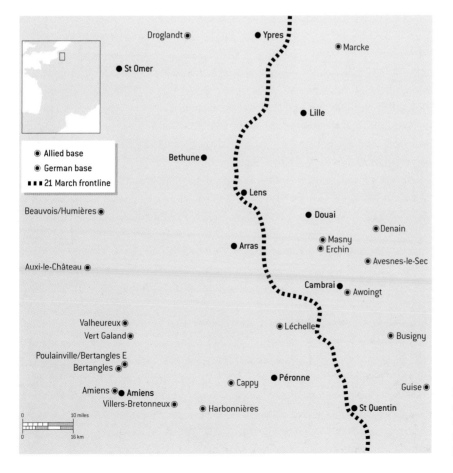

British and German fighter airfields during the *Kaiserschlact* spring offensive, launched on 21 March 1918.

Ltn Johannes Werner's Albatros D Va and new Dr I 198/17 both display his variation on Jasta 14's black and white bands along the fuselage side in January 1918. Thanks largely to Werner, Jasta 14 did not have to relinquish its Dr Is to Jagdgeschwader II. Indeed, the unit flew them longer than most Staffeln, with examples remaining in service with the Jasta months after superior Fokker D VIIs became available in significant numbers. (Greg VanWyngarden)

Anticipating their arrival, von Richthofen hedged his bets by accepting Dr Is for Jastas 6 and 11, while retaining Albatros D Vs and Pfalz D IIIs as the principal equipment for Jastas 4 and 10. Likewise, Berthold had let Jastas 12, 13 and 19 keep their triplanes, but had perpetrated a unique swap between Jasta 15 and his old unit, Jasta 18, in both personnel and aircraft.

In consequence Jasta 15's triplanes were replaced by Jasta 18's Albatros D Vs, complete with the blue tails and red engine cowlings, based on regimental dress uniform sleeves and cuffs favoured by Berthold, to form a common marking theme that would later be adopted throughout JG II. In contrast, Loerzer intended all four of JG III's Staffeln to use Dr Is, although there were only enough immediately available for Jastas Boelcke and 36, Jastas 26 and 27 having to continue operating their Albatros D Vs well into March.

An odd unit out was Jasta 14, which got Dr Is in January, but due to personality differences between its commander, Ltn Johannes Werner, and Hptm von Tutschek, never joined JG II as originally planned. Even so, although 'Hans' Werner probably had to fight for the privilege, his Staffel still had its triplanes on 19 March, when it moved to Masny aerodrome, north of Erchin, to support the XVII Armee in the coming offensive.

On the British side of the lines Camel squadrons were well established all along the front. Moreover, coincidental with the Fokker F I's stunning, but short-lived, combat debut, the Camels saw their first use in a role that underlined the Germans' need for air superiority if their offensive was to succeed. On 19 September 1917, Nos 70 Sqn RFC and 10 Sqn RNAS conducted the first organized ground attack mission by Camels when they strafed a number of German trenches and troop positions all along the Ypres front.

After the capture of Passchendaele on 6 November 1917, the British prepared to shift their offensive in Flanders toward Cambrai. One day later, Lt Arthur Gould Lee recorded the arrival of the first Camel to No. 46 Sqn RFC, and his first flight in the Sopwith fighter the following day:

First impressions – more room in the cockpit, so you can take a deep breath without feeling you're going to burst the fuselage at the seams (but why on earth didn't they fit it with a parachute?). Second, the exciting pull of the 130hp Clerget, and the surge of power at full throttle. Third, her amazing lightness on the controls, lighter even than a Pup, which is gentle-sensitive, while the Camel is fierce, razor sharp. She turns with lightning quickness to the right. You have to be careful taking off as the engine torque veers her to the left, and you have to apply full right rudder, but it's easy enough once you get the knack. I've not fired the guns yet, that's a pleasure to come.

Our one Camel has been taking off and landing all day as a succession of pilots tried their hand. Marvellously, nobody has broken it.

On 9 November, Lee noted the other trend that attended his unit's Pup replacements:

My other flying was a low cross-country, and bomb-dropping practice. We were actually ordered to do the low-level flight, which normally is officially frowned on. Our machines have been fitted with racks under the fuselage to carry four 20lb bombs, and a target has been laid out on the aerodrome on which we release our dummy bombs. I wonder what's afoot?

On 10 November Lee was confident enough to stunt in the Camel, and noted some further impressions in his diary:

She loops practically automatically, as she is tail heavy – so much so that in level flying you have to press against the joystick the whole time. Result, if you don't press, she just goes up and over. But you have to watch your rudder. She does a very fast flick-roll – on the Pup this calls for a certain knack, but the Camel goes round effortlessly and instantly.

This Camel has been fitted with an underfuselage rack to allow it to carry 25lb Cooper bombs. The British pressed the Camel into the trench-strafing role in late September 1917, regarding its agility as an asset for dodging ground fire. (Museum of Flight Peter Bowers Collection)

On 17 November Lee was issued with his very own Camel, B2501, and he used it to continue bomb-dropping practice:

> You dive at the target until you're at about 100ft, meanwhile judging the exact moment to release the bomb with the control on the joystick. Pretending you're on the real job, you then flatten out and swerve quickly aside to get clear of the upward burst of the explosion. Dropping dummies on the aerodrome target, with no bullets to bother me, I found it surprisingly easy to get close results. In fact mine were much the best in the squadron. My proudest four, dropped one at a time, were all within a yard or two of the target, compared with other people's 100 yards, and one man's 170 yards. I hope this unexpected skill doesn't land me into any awkward jobs. It was a thrilling experience to shoot with two guns for the first time – the whole machine shudders with the rapid rate-of-fire and the double explosions.

After leading his first Camel patrol on the 19th and attacking some Albatros D Vs, Lee wrote of the thrill he got from the shrieking wires as his aeroplane dived at 140mph, but also noted that:

Lt Arthur Stanley Gould Lee of No.46 Sqn RFC was among the first Camel pilots to encounter the Red Baron's triplane. He was also an early trainee in the art of ground attack in Camels.
(Jon Guttman)

> The Albatros dives fast too, and we can't catch them up. I also find the Camel tiring to fly in formation for a long patrol. She's so sensitive you can't relax for a second, and you have the contant pressure on the joystick, which in two hours' flying makes your right arm ache. But she's such a marvellous aeroplane these handicaps are unimportant.
>
> But imagine after waiting all those months for Camels, striving not to be shot down in Pups, and looking forward to toppling Huns two at a time with my two Vickers, to find myself switched to ground strafing!

By mid-March 1918, a total of 336 Camels in 15 squadrons – Nos 3, 43, 46, 54, 65, 73 and 80, No. 4 Sqn Australian Flying Corps (AFC), and Nos 1, 3, 4, 8, 9, 10 and 13 RNAS – were stationed at aerodromes along the Western Front. Three others – Nos 28, 45 and 66 RFC – had been transferred to Italy as part of a general Anglo-French effort to bolster their Italian ally in the wake of Caporetto. For comparison, Fokker Dr I strength along the Western Front would peak in April 1918 at 171.

THE COMBATANTS

Comparing statistics, airframe characteristics and engine reliability tends to give the Sopwith F 1 Camel an overall edge over the Fokker Dr I in a one-on-one dogfight, given pilots of equal skill. Such an ideal scenario, however, was seldom realized in the spring of 1918, when Camel units were a mixed bag of 'old hands' and newly arrived trainees, whereas the Luftstreitskräfte, in anticipation of the *Kaiserschlacht*, allotted most of its handful of Dr Is to pilots of proven proficiency in JGs I, II and III.

CAMEL PILOTS

Although generally typical of the newer Camel pilots, Mark Curtis Kinney was exceptional in two respects – he was an American from Mount Vernon, Ohio, who, after being rejected by the US Army because of inadequate hearing in his left ear, had enlisted in the RFC at age 30. This made him downright ancient compared to most of his contemporaries, whose ages ranged from late teens to mid-20s.

After swearing allegiance to King George V, Kinney began training at Long Branch Camp, north of Toronto, Canada, on 3 August 1917. At nearby Armour Heights Aerodrome on 23 September, he made his first flight in a Curtiss JN 4. Kinney soloed on 9 October, and after further training in Texas, he returned to Toronto to get his wings and his second lieutenant's commission on 27 November.

Kinney was subsequently shipped to England, and from 7 January 1918, he logged ten hours in Avro 504s at No. 10 Training Squadron at Shawbury Flying Camp. On the 25th he moved on to Pups, and soon after that mastered the Camel with relative ease. Kinney wrote in his memoir, *I Flew a Camel*:

I liked its quick response – it was so remarkably swift and sensitive that it demanded
constant attention. The torque caused the nose to rise in a left-hand turn and drop in a
right-hand turn. Fairly large amounts of left rudder were needed in both turns to correct
for these idiosyncrasies. The tiny biplane was so sensitive in a turn, however, that if the
turn were tightened just a little, it was likely to whip into a tight spin – quickly and
without warning. Oddly, this very ease for spinning was used in combat by many pilots
to shake a persistent German from their tails.

A quick-witted, cool-headed pilot could turn the Camel's sensitivity from a liability
to an asset. Scottish ace Norman MacMillan saw a pupil spin right in one, overcorrect
and spin left, overcorrect again and still recover from the resultant right-hand spin
and land safely. 'What other aeroplane ever built', MacMillan asked, 'could do all that
in under 1000ft?'

On 6 March 1918, Kinney and Canadian 2Lt Lorne H. McIntyre, who he had
befriended in training, reported to the Pilot's Pool near Paris-Plage. 'We were thinking
the same thoughts – that somewhere in France a British squadron would call for
replacements', Kinney recalled. 'Two pilots would be shot down, or taken prisoner,
and we would fill their empty chairs at the squadron mess'.

A few days later a lorry transported Kinney and McIntyre to No. 3 Sqn RFC at
Worloy. Both were assigned to 'A' Flight under Capt Cyril M. Leman, who conducted
six familiarization flights before committing them to regular patrols. 'He took us up
to 6000ft and put his nose down with engine full on', Kinney said of one such sortie.
'We were expected to stay with him in V formation. Lorne and I took the challenge
and stuck right with him. Before Leman straightened out, my ear drums felt as though
they would crack due to the rapid pressure change. But I got over it, and I never
mentioned my ear discomfort to anyone'.

Another 'natural pilot' who made an unusually swift transition into a Camel was
1Lt George A. Vaughn Jr, an American who had scored seven victories flying SE 5as

with No. 84 Sqn RFC prior to joining the 17th Aero Squadron – one of two USAS Camel units attached to No. 65 Wing RAF at Auxi-le-Château on 26 August 1918.

Vaughn described his previous Pup training as being more suitable for the SE 5a than the Camel, yet in the process of taking off on his first Camel flight, he immediately felt out the stick and rudder action necessary to control the Sopwith fighter. Vaughn gave the Camel qualified praise:

> Although inherently unstable – rigged so tail heavy that it could nose up and stall immediately if flown hands off – it was highly manoeuvrable, climbed well at low and medium altitudes and, when properly handled, was a most effective weapon for close-in air combat at these altitudes.

Even so, he preferred the SE 5a's speed, as well as its less draughty, more comfortable cockpit and the long exhaust pipes on which he would alternately place his gloved hands to warm them at altitude.

'Not even the Fokker triplane could follow a Camel in a right-handed bank', affirmed Capt Henry Winslow Woollett, a pre-war medical student from Southwold, Suffolk, who had scored five victories in de Havilland DH 2s and DH 5s with No. 24 Sqn RFC before joining No. 43 Sqn RFC in March 1918. Still, he agreed with another pilot's quip that one 'had to shoot down all the Huns to get home himself, for there was no chance to run for it'.

A seasoned flight leader and respected 'old man' at age 22, Woollett described No. 43 Sqn's men as a 'wonderful lot of young and full-out pilots, lively and

The skills of Camel pilots varied widely. B5663 of No. 10 Sqn RNAS had been used by Flt Cdr Wilfred A. Curtis to score his 11th victory on 5 December 1917, but on 23 January 1918, Flt Sub-Lt Ross A. Blythe – who had joined Curtis' 'A' Flight just ten days earlier – was flying it when he collided with an Albatros D V, killing himself and his opponent, Ltn Gustav Wandelt of Jasta 36. (Greg VanWyngarden)

WILLIAM L. JORDAN

Among the lesser-known aces of World War I, William Lancelot Jordan was credited with the most triplanes downed by any Camel pilot. Born in Georgetown, South Africa, on 3 December 1896, he was living in London when war broke out and enlisted in the RNAS as an air mechanic. From there he became an air gunner, and eventually moved on to pilot training and was posted to No. 8 Sqn RNAS. By July 1917 the unit had replaced its Sopwith Triplanes with Camels, and on the 13th Jordan downed a Rumpler two-seater out of control for his first victory.

On 11 August Jordan and Flt Cdr Charles Dawson Booker shared in the destruction of a black Albatros D V near Acheville, this aircraft having been flown by Oblt Adolf Ritter von Tutschek of Jasta 12, who had 23 victories to his credit at this time. Badly wounded in the shoulder, von Tutschek would later command JG II and claim four more victories in Fokker Dr Is before being killed on 15 March 1918. Jordan scored his ninth victory – an Albatros D V – in concert with Flt Sub-Lt Edward G Johnstone and Flt Sub-Lt Reid on New Year's Day 1918, and his tally stood at 20 by mid-April, when he was promoted to the rank of captain in the newly formed RAF.

Jordan claimed his first Dr I out of control on 23 May. While the German fighter was credited as his 24th victory, it is likely that the triplane pilot he outfought had, as was often the case, managed to convince Jordan and attendant Allied witnesses that his aircraft was in more distress than it really was. The same may not be said, however, for another Dr I that Jordan, along with Lts R. L. Johns, P. M. Dennett and J. S. McDonald, drove down out of control near Merville. Their victim was Ltn Hans Grabe of Jasta 14, who died of his wounds on 7 June. Jordan was awarded the DFC soon after.

His next triplane claims came on 7 July, some two miles east of La Bassée, and at 0750hrs the following day between Meurchin and Epinoy, followed by a Pfalz D IIIa ten minutes later. By then the triplane had passed its prime, and the second-string Jastas to which Dr Is had been passed down were struggling to keep their engines from burning up the castor oil substitute Voltol and seizing in the summer heat. Again, however, there are no corresponding German casualties for these claims, nor was there one for the Dr I Jordan sent down out of control over Meurchin on 7 August. One might speculate that his opponents could have simply spun down rather than risk a protracted dogfight with unreliable engines.

Jordan's last success was an LVG out of control 1.5 miles north-east of Pacaut Wood on 12 August, after which he returned to the UK on rest leave. Twenty of his 39 accredited victories were shared, and five were over triplanes. Jordan was killed in a car crash in late 1931.

WILLIAM S. STEPHENSON

Being second among Camel pilots credited with Dr Is shot down is the least of William Samuel Stephenson's claims to fame. Born in Winnepeg, British Columbia, on 11 January 1896, he began the war in the Winnipeg Light Infantry, served as an engineer and survived being gassed in 1916. Stephenson applied to the RFC on 16 August 1917 and joined No. 73 Sqn on 9 February 1918. He scored his first victory over an Albatros D V on 22 March, followed by an LVG in flames two days later.

On 3 May Stephenson was credited with a Dr I near Ploegsteert – possibly from Jasta Boelcke, although the pilot survived – but his next such claim did not come until 9 July, west of Moncheaux. Twelve days later he shared in the destruction of a Dr I north-east of Oulchy le Château with Maj R. H. Freeman, Capt M. LeBlanc Smith, Lt G. L. Graham, 2Lt K. S. Laurie, Lt W. Sidebottom, 2Lt R. N. Chandler, Lt J. Balfour and Lt W. G. Peters. Their opponents were apparently from Jasta 36, which lost no pilots, whereas Ltn Harry von Bülow killed No. 73 Sqn's commander, Maj Freeman. Stephenson claimed his fourth triplane, as well as a Fokker D VII over Bazoches, the following day.

After sharing in the destruction of an LVG on 25 July, Stephenson went missing three days later. He was last seen battling seven Fokker D VIIs, one of which went down in flames for his 12th victory. The Germans credited him to Ltn Justus Grassmann of Jasta 10, but Stephenson later claimed that after disengaging from the dogfight he drove some Germans away from a French two-seater, only to be shot in the left leg by its gunner, and as he came down over German lines, he was hit again by a machine gunner, force-landed and was taken prisoner.

Stephenson later escaped from the POW camp in which he was incarcerated, taking note of every German installation of possible military value as he made his way back to rejoin his squadron. In addition to the Military Cross, Stephenson was gazetted for the Distinguished Flying Cross in a citation that prophetically read, in part, 'His reports, also, have contained valuable and accurate information'.

Moving to England in 1924, Stephenson became a wealthy industrialist whose international business dealings allowed him to acquire information on Nazi rearmament in circumvention of the Treaty of Versailles, which he started passing on to opposition MP Winston Churchill as early as April 1936. In World War II he rose to prominence in the counterintelligence role in North America using the codename 'Intrepid'. Knighted by King George VI and awarded the Presidential Medal for Merit by the Americans, in 1976 he wrote a best-selling autobiography, *A Man Called Intrepid*.

Stephenson died in Paget, Bermuda, in January 1989. Ian Fleming, who used him as the model for 'spymaster M' in his novels, summed his career up in 1962 when he wrote 'James Bond is a highly romanticised version of a true spy. The real thing is William Stephenson'.

enthuasiastic', yet there 'was no glory bagger who flew without regard for his flight'. He extended that admiration to the squadron's riggers, fitters and armourers:

> We owed them everything for what they did for us. We were entirely in their hands, and what reward did they get out of the war? In my own case just my appreciation for what they did for me, and the knowledge that our war in the air was won through their absolute help in looking after my safety and my guns.

Woollett survived the war with 35 victories, including six on 6 April 1918, although none was over a Dr I.

Ronald Adam of No. 73 Sqn RFC described how a typical Camel pilot prepared for battle:

> I began to put on my overall suit, pull up my heavy sheepskin thighboots and to wrap a woollen muffler around my neck. Then, with the addition of a fur-lined

Claiming 54 victories, Donald R. MacLaren of No. 46 Sqn RAF was the top Camel ace. He is seen here with an aeroplane whose upper wing cutout was enlarged for better visibility. 'I had several encounters with Fokker triplanes in July or August 1918', he said. 'It was a highly manoeuvrable opponent, but could not take steep dives and was not more manoeuvrable than the Sopwith Camel 110hp Le Rhône or 150hp Bentley. It could usually out-climb us, but its ceiling was no higher than the Bentley Camel – 10,000ft indicated by aneroid, although this was probably about 14,000ft, which was the physical pilot limit'. (Jon Guttman)

helmet, fur-lined face mask and goggles, and a pair of silk gloves underneath my lambsfleece flying gloves, I was ready. While the mechanics continued to work on my machine, I put chocolate in my pockets and swallowed the peculiar breakfast my batman had brought to me – a piece of fat bacon, a bottle of cold tea and an orange. I loaded my Very pistol and placed it in a handy position inside the cockpit, with some spare cartridges in my breast pocket.

DREIDECKERFLIEGER

The German airman in 1918 wore specially issued *Fliegerhosen* in combination with whatever protective jacket he could obtain, but many photographs reveal his preference for enemy apparel whenever he could bring an *Englander* down unhurt. One-piece Sidney Cotton suits, or 'Sidcots', long brown leather coats and fleece-lined gloves and 'fug boots' appropriated from a captured 'Lord' were not mere trophies, but prized items for personal use.

One exclusively German piece of equipment in 1918 was a parachute, held in place by a Heinecke harness reinforced with leather and broad leg straps. Released by a tether attached inside the cockpit as the pilot bailed out, German 'chutes were bulky and frequently prone to failure, but they did save lives. Allied commanders resisted issuing such devices because they thought that they would encourage airmen to abandon their aeroplanes prematurely. The Luftstreitskräfte, wishing to conserve its limited resource of trained men, soon discovered that while parachutes enhanced their confidence, German pilots still preferred trying to bring their stricken aeroplanes down for a forced landing if possible, using their unreliable parachutes as a last resort.

The collective talent of the Jagdgeschwader pilots notwithstanding, all but a handful of pioneer Eindecker and Fokker D II and D III pilots had cut their teeth on heavier aircraft powered by inline, water-cooled engines, such as the Albatros D III and D V, and Pfalz D III. Consequently, the first indication that a *Jagdstaffel* fighter squadron was slated to re-equip with triplanes was the arrival of Fokker D Vs, whose airframe structure harkened to late 1916 – obsolescent before they entered production, but ideal as fighter trainers to re-accustom a new generation of pilots to rotary-engined flight.

Once they had done some time on the Fokker D V, German pilots moved on to the Dr I – an experience rather similar to that of their British counterparts transitioning from Pup to Camel. Unlike the Sopwith Triplane, whose middle wing, situated level with the pilot's eye, interfered little with visibility, the Fokker's middle wing was flush with the upper fuselage decking, necessitating a cutout to improve the pilot's downward view – and even that was further impeded by the lower wing. Consequently, a Dr I was more difficult to land than a Camel, requiring the pilot to gauge his proximity to the ground during final approach from the side, or even by jinking sideways just before his wheels touched the turf. That, plus the omnipresent engine torque, explains why Fokker installed underwing skids on production Dr Is to minimize damage from ground-loops.

Ltn Ernst Udet had scored 20 victories in Albatros D IIIs and D Vs when Manfred von Richthofen invited him to relinquish his command of Jasta 37 and join JG I. Upon Udet's arrival at Awoingt aerodrome at 1000hrs on 15 March 1918, von Richthofen had him fly the noon patrol. 'He puts great store in personally trying out

From left, Uffz Robert Eiserbeck, Ltn Hans Weiss and Vzfw Edgar Scholtz of Jasta 11 stand before Dr Is flown by Ltns Richard Wenzl (with black and white band) and Eberhardt Mohnicke (with swastika) at Léchelle in early April 1918. By the time this photograph was taken, Mohnicke had already been wounded on 1 March, while Eiserbeck would fatally crash into a hillside south of Méault on 12 April and Weiss and Scholtz would perish in combat on 2 May. (Alex Imrie)

HANS KIRSCHSTEIN

Although the vast majority of his 80 victories were scored in Albatros D IIIs and D Vs, Manfred von Richthofen is justly associated with the Fokker triplane for the final 20 successes that he achieved while flying that type. Included in that number are eight Camels. Ltn Hans Kirschstein was another outstanding Dr I exponent in the Baron's Circus, 15 of his 27 victories – including six Camels – being scored with the Dr I.

Born in Koblenz on 5 August 1896, Kirschstein served in the 3rd Pioneer Battalion in France and Galicia (he developed malaria in the latter location) until May 1917, when he transferred into aviation. Assigned to Flieger Abteilung 19, he took part in a bombing raid on Dover and strafed British tanks over Flanders. Kirschstein subsequently flew with Fl Abt 256 and Fl Abt 3, before joining Jasta 6 on 13 March 1918. He scored his first victory – a Camel flown by Capt F. L. Luxmoore, commander of No. 54 Sqn RFC – five days later. On the 27th Kirschstein downed a two-seat Armstrong Whitworth FK 8 of No. 2 Sqn RFC and a Camel, probably from No. 73 Sqn RFC.

On 6 April, Kirschstein brought down a Camel from No. 3 Sqn RAF, 2Lt D. G. Gold being taken POW, and the next day he similarly downed Lt Ronald G. H. Adams of No. 73 Sqn RAF, who would survive captivity to become actor Ronald Adam post-war.

On 10 May Jasta 6 caught No. 80 Sqn's Camels on a strafing mission at Chipilly and claimed three, resulting in two deaths – Kirschstein's victim was 2Lt G. A. Wateley. His last Camel claim fell east of Demuin on 15 May, killing Lt G. Wilson of No. 209 Sqn RAF, and he added two Bristol F 2Bs to his tally during the course of the day.

Jasta 6 identified itself within JG I by black and white tailplane bands, but Kirschstein extended that motif to the after part of the fuselage, the upper wing and the interplane struts of his Dr I 586/17 in a diagonal manner that Staffel mate Ltn Richard Wenzl called an 'optische Täuschung', or optical illusion.

Switching to the Fokker D VII – which he completely overpainted in his diagonal black and white 'optische Täuschung' bands – Kirschstein had raised his tally to 24 by the time he was given command of Jasta 6 on 10 June. Exactly two weeks later, in addition to receiving the Orden Pour le Mérite, Kirschstein downed a Breguet 14 for his 27th victory.

On 16 July Kirschstein flew his D VII to the aircraft park at Fismes for overhaul and Ltn Johannes Markgraf, who had joined the Staffel only five days earlier, arrived to fly him back to Jasta 6 in a Hannover CL II. 'Kirschstein, who couldn't wait to get going, climbed in behind the novice pilot', Ltn Wenzl recalled. 'Markgraf, who had little experience in the Hannover, over-controlled the machine. They crashed from an altitude of 50 metres and died soon after. Kirschstein's death hit us all very hard'.

JOSEF JACOBS

Arguably the most diehard – and successful – Fokker Dr I pilot of them all, Josef Carl Peter Jacobs was born in Kreuzkapelle, Rhineland, on 15 May 1894. Learning to fly in 1912, he had served in the Luftstreitskräfte from the outbreak of war and scored his first two victories in the spring of 1916 while flying in Fokker Staffel West. In November Jacobs transferred to Jagdstaffel 22, commanded by his friend Oblt Erich Honemanns, and also instructed at Jastaschule I through the winter of 1916–17. On 2 August 1917 Ltn Jacobs, with five victories, was given command of Jasta 7.

In early 1918 Jacobs received his first Dr I, and he became so enamoured with it that he would keep at least two on hand, even after acquiring one of the faster D VIIs, until at least October 1918. His stated means of overcoming the triplane's engine problems was to replace inoperative engines outright from a pool of British rotaries recovered from downed Camels, often provided by frontline troops in exchange for Jacobs' standing offer of a case of champagne for each reparable specimen.

Jacobs' tally has been variously described as 44 or 48, and more than 30 of those victories – including 11 Camels – were scored in Dr Is, although relatively few of them are supported by a documented Allied loss. One exception occurred on 5 June, when he shot down Camel B7229 of No. 203 Sqn RAF, killing Flt Sub-Lt A. N. Webster. 'We were flying over the front near Bailleul, when I saw some flak burst above Bral de Nieppe', Jacobs reported. 'I accelerated my triplane and saw some additional ack-ack bursts near our balloon line. I pulled up my nose again and spotted four Camels coming toward our front. I stood my tripe on its nose and fired one long burst until the Camel started smoking, so I rolled over onto the second one who entangled me in a wild dogfight, during which he shot my tail to pieces. I evaded his firing and went after the first Camel again, which soon went all the way down and crashed'.

On 26 June Jacobs claimed a Camel near Menin, whose pilot 'had fought very courageously'. 2Lt C. D. Boothman, a 19-year-old Camel pilot of No. 210 Sqn RAF, was killed.

Jacobs preserved a lively log of his missions and exploits, which included surviving two mid-air collisions. He was awarded the Orden Pour le Mérite on 18 July 1918.

After the war Jacobs fought communists in the Baltic Sea region, was a flight instructor for the Turkish army, was a director of the Adler Werke and owned an aircraft manufacturing plant in Erfurt. After Adolf Hitler came to power in 1933, Jacobs made no secret of his anti-Nazi sentiments, and although commissioned as a Major der Reserve, he declined service in the new Luftwaffe. Moving to the Netherlands and spending some of World War II in hiding, Jacobs returned to Bavaria after the conflict and died in Munich on 29 July 1978.

each new man', Udet wrote, also noting, 'For the first time I fly the Fokker triplane'. During another sortie that same afternoon, von Richthofen reported:

> With five gentlemen of Jagdstaffel 11 at low altitude, Ltn Udet and I encountered a Sopwith single-seater. At the beginning of the fight the opponent attempted to escape by skillful flying. I fired from an aeroplane's length away and set him on fire. During the fall it broke up into pieces, with the fuselage falling into the small wood of Contalmaison.

A Fokker D V in flight. These fighter trainers provided German Jagdstaffeln slated to receive Dr Is with an introduction to rotary engined aircraft prior to flying the triplanes. (Jon Guttman)

The Baron's hapless victim, 2Lt Donald Cameron of No. 3 Sqn RFC, was on a trench-strafing mission, and his still-attached bombs exploded when his Camel hit the ground.

Udet quickly mastered the Dr I, and two days later he downed an RE 8 near Albert. When he landed, a smiling von Richthofen enquired, 'Do you always bring them down with frontal attacks, Udet?' 'I have had repeated success that way', Udet replied as nonchalantly as possible. Turning to go, von Richthofen off-handedly added over his shoulder, 'By the way, you can take charge of Jasta 11 starting tomorrow'.

While most Jastas were quartered in towns or buildings 20 or 30 kilometres behind the frontlines, Udet observed, 'The von Richthofen group dwells in corrugated shacks that can be erected and broken down in a matter of hours', and was seldom more than 20 kilometres from the front. 'Other squadrons go up two or three times a day', he added. 'Von Richthofen and his men fly five times a day. Others close down operations in bad weather, but here they fly under almost any condition'.

The greatest surprise to Udet, however, was the forward airstrips JG I established. He wrote:

> Just a few kilometres behind the lines, often within range of the enemy artillery, we are on fully dressed standby, lounging in reclining chairs in an open field. Our aircraft, gassed up and ready to go, are right alongside. As soon as an opponent appears on the horizon, we go up – one, two or an entire Staffel. Immediately, after the fight we land, stretch out in our reclining chairs, and scour the sky with binoculars, waiting for the next opponent. Standing patrols are not flown. Von Richthofen doesn't believe in them. He'll allow only patrols into the enemy's rear areas. 'This business of standing sentry duty in the air weakens the pilots' will to fight', he maintains. Thus we only go up to fight.

COMBAT

The first victory for a Fokker Dr I – as distinguished from the F I – occurred on 13 January 1918, when Ltn Werner Steinhäuser burned a British balloon at Hendrecourt. Jasta 11's first success of the year was soured, however, when one of Steinhäuser's partners, Ltn Eberhardt Stapenhorst, was brought down by ground fire, both he and his Dr I 144/17 falling into British hands intact. The thorough evaluation that followed ended any remaining claim the Fokker triplane had to 'secret weapon' status.

On 3 February Vzfw Otto Fruhner of Jasta 26 claimed a Camel over Poelkappelle at 1145hrs, although the British recorded no losses to triplanes that morning. That afternoon, Jasta 26 engaged Camels of No. 9 Sqn RNAS, and Flt Cdr R. R. Winter was credited with a triplane. Moments later, however, his wings folded and he crashed to his death. Jasta 26 reported no losses, but managed to out-overclaim the British this time by crediting another Camel to Fruhner and three to OffStv Otto Esswein.

Jasta 11 suffered another disturbing setback that same day when Ltn Hans-Joachim Wolff force-landed after the spar and the leading edge of his upper wing collapsed. Further, on the 27th von Richthofen wrote to Oblt Fritz von Falkenhayn, technical officer to the Luftstreistkräfte's general staff, complaining of the poor quality of the Rizinus-Ersatz lubricant in the Dr Is' rotaries, and reiterating his preference for Fokker D VIIs with BMW or supercharged Mercedes water-cooled engines. 'Should the Fokkers be issued with unsupercharged engines', he added, 'I would not refuse them'.

On 6 March, Ltn Erich Bahr of Jasta 11 was killed between Nauroy and Etricourt by Camel pilot Capt A. H. G. Fellowes of No. 54 Sqn RFC. Aerial skirmishing escalated as the British became aware of the coming onslaught and, as usual, sent patrols over enemy lines. On 8 March Ltn Hans von Haebler of Jasta 36 downed Camel B3906 between Roulers and Menin, Flt Sub-Lt H. R. Casgrain of No. 12 Sqn RNAS becoming a POW.

Ltn Werner Steinhäuser of Jasta 11, seen beside his Dr I 564/17 at Cappy in late April 1918, burned a balloon over Hendrecourt on 13 January, 1918. That first Fokker Dr I success was offset, however, by the capture of Ltn Eberhardt Stapenhorst and his Dr I 144/17 after they were brought down by ground fire that same day. (Greg VanWyngarden)

On 9 March Lt Guy M. Knocker of No. 65 Sqn RFC recorded an offensive patrol, flown between 1000hrs and 1115hrs, in his flight log;

Our first experience of the Fokker triplane. Five of them dived on the front lot. We went at four of them but did not get them. I shot at one diving on another Camel, whereon all four transferred their attention to me. I faded away. Cox and Brembridge both got one today.

Apparently, No. 65 Sqn had had a run-in with triplanes from JG III, and for a change the Germans seem to have had the worst of it. Of the two Dr Is credited to Knocker's squadronmates, Lts G. Bembridge and G. M. Cox, the latter's stalled and went into a spin, during which one of its wings folded up. Cox's victim was probably Ltn Max Naujock of Jasta 36, who was wounded in the lungs and died en route to the hospital. On the other hand, Knocker's might have been the Camel claimed in the fight by Vzfw Paul Bäumer of Jasta Boelcke, for which no identifiable loss has turned up on the British side.

Knocker, who self-effacingly called himself 'a completely undistinguished Camel pilot', described No. 65 Sqn's Camels as being equipped with 130hp and later 160hp Clerget engines, although some were later fitted with 'Bentley Rotary 1 engines – a great improvement. The Camel had a top speed of about 110mph low down. It was extremely manoeuvrable and very light on fore-and-aft control. The rotary engine had a considerable gyroscopic effect so that you required full left rudder on both vertical turns and loops. A Camel was a very cold aeroplane, and it had an endearing habit of soaking your right foot in engine oil. Although it was not as good very high up as its predecessor the Pup, those of us who mastered the Camel thought there was no other aircraft quite like it. It could turn on a sixpence and you could put it down on a dinner plate'.

Another encounter between Camel and Dr I on 9 March involved a patrol led by Capt Sharpe of No. 73 Sqn RFC, which encountered five Albatros D Vs led by a triplane near St Quentin at 1140hrs. The Fokker turned in behind the patrol and Thomas Sydney Sharpe responded by attacking the Dr I, which then spun down until it disappeared in the ground haze.

At 1420hrs on March 10, Vzfw Franz Hemer of Jasta 6 brought a Camel down at Montbrehain, with 2Lt C. H. Flere of No. 80 Sqn RFC being taken prisoner. Five minutes later, five Dr Is of Jasta 6 dived on a flight of No. 73 Sqn RFC Camels, led by Capt Maurice LeBlanc-Smith, at 13,500ft west of Bohain. Smith turned to engage one, fired at a range of 75yds and saw the Fokker spin away. He repeated the performance with a second, which Lts George Stacey Hodson and T. G. Drew-Brook reported to have seen hit the ground. Hodson spotted another triplane 1,000ft below him, dived to within 100yds of it and opened fire. His quarry reportedly went into a nosedive, during which its wings folded back and ripped off. Smith's and Hodson's confirmed victories were also the first for their squadron, but Jasta 6's only casualty that day was Uffz Paul Beschow, most likely wounded by Hodson.

Capt Orlando C. Bridgeman of No. 80 Sqn RFC claimed two triplanes over Morcourt four hours later, but there was no matching German loss for them, nor for the Dr I claimed by Capt Thomas Sydney Sharpe of No. 73 Sqn RFC the next day.

On 13 March DH 4s of Nos 25 and 27 Sqns bombed Denain aerodrome, escorted by two flights of No. 73 Sqn RFC Camels and 11 Bristol F 2Bs of No. 62 Sqn

Vzfws Fritz Classen (left) and Otto Fruhner and Offstv Otto Esswein of Jasta 26 pose in front of the latter's Dr I 426/17, which has yet to have his initial 'E' applied. Fruhner claimed the first two Camels to fall to a Dr I pilot, and Esswein three more, on 3 February 1918. (Greg VanWyngarden)

Camels of No. 73 Sqn RAF at an airstrip near Humières on 6 April 1918, with a Bristol F 2B landing in the background. Airmen in both aircraft claimed to have downed Ltn Lothar von Richthofen's Dr I during the dogfight of 13 March 1918. (Greg VanWyngarden)

RFC – the latter having been mauled by Jasta 11 the day before. They were intercepted by Dr Is of JG I and Albatros D Vas of Jasta 56, and the scrap drew in patrolling SE 5as of No. 24 Sqn RFC. Jasta 56 accounted for two Bristols and an SE 5a, while Hemer of Jasta 6 claimed another SE 5a and Manfred von Richthofen drove down a Camel, its pilot, Lt Elmer E. Heath, being wounded and taken POW.

Multiple claiming prevailed on the British side, but Ltn Walter Bowien of Jasta 56 was killed and Lothar von Richthofen crash-landed, suffering facial injuries that put him out of the war until July. Both Germans were credited to Camels and Bristols, the former's claimants being No. 73 Sqn's Lt George S. Hodson over a red-coloured Albatros that crashed near Wambai and Capt Augustus H. Orlebar over a triplane which he reported as diving with its top plane coming off, as well as another Albatros out of control. The day ended on a sober note for No. 73 Sqn RFC when Vzfw Edgar Scholtz of Jasta 11 killed 2Lt J. N. L. Millet in flames over Vaucelles at 1440hrs.

On 18 March 'Naval 5's' DH 4s flew another bombing mission, this time to Busigny aerodrome, with No. 54 Sqn's Camels and No. 84's SE 5as in attendance. The British aircraft stirred up a bigger hornets' nest than they had on the 13th in the form of some 50 fighters from Jastas 3, 4, 5, 6, 10, 11, 16b, 34b, 37, 46, 54 and 56, all led by von Richthofen. In the sprawling air battle, No.84 Sqn RFC claimed seven victories, including two triplanes, and No. 54 Sqn's two successes included a triplane in flames by 2Lt E. A. Richardson.

The Germans admitted to four aeroplanes lost and three pilots killed, none of them in Dr Is, while claiming a DH 4, two Bristols of No. 11 Sqn, a Breguet 14, an SE 5a and eight Camels. "Naval 5" lost a DH 4 with its crew, and No. 84 Sqn's 2Lt John A. McCudden, brother of James McCudden, was killed by Ltn Wolff. No. 54 Sqn RFC lost a staggering five Camels, including 2Lt William G. Ivamy, taken prisoner after being driven down by von Richthofen, 2Lt E. B. Lee, brought down as a POW by Scholtz, and the squadron commander, Capt F. L. Luxmoore, also captured following combat with Ltn Hans Kirschstein of Jasta 6. Elsewhere, Ltn Haebler of Jasta 36 shot down a Camel of 'Naval 3', killing Flt Sub-Lt J. L. Allison.

Capt Francis M. Kitto, a flight leader in No. 54 Sqn, summed the mission up in a subsequent telephone conversation with 'Naval 5'. 'Frightful affair ... frightful affair!' Frightful affair as it seemed, the escalating aerial activities of the past weeks had been mere preliminaries. The main event was about to begin.

The German offensive, Operation *Michael*, began on 21 March, with an artillery barrage of unprecedented intensity, followed by an onslaught of specially trained storm troopers, as the German 17., 2. and 18. Armees assaulted the British Fifth Army and the right wing of the Third. Bad weather limited aerial activity, and the Dr Is were seldom seen compared to the Camels, whose pilots were patrolling the skies or strafing enemy ground troops whenever the meteorological vagaries permitted. JG III was more in evidence on the 22nd, with Fritz Loerzer and Otto Esswein of Jasta 26 claiming Camels of No. 70 Sqn RFC at 1555hrs. Ltn Heinrich Bongartz of Jasta 36 downed a Camel of No. 46 Sqn RFC near Lagnicourt on the 23rd, while both Bruno and Fritz Loerzer were credited with Camels whose identity and true fate cannot be ascertained. JG I's pilots were also up, usually in Geschwader strength, whenever the weather cleared a bit, flying 80 sorties during the course of the day but accomplishing little or nothing for their effort.

Von Richthofen destroyed an SE 5a on the 24th, and the next day he felled another Camel near Contalmaison, killing 2Lt Donald Cameron of No. 3 Sqn RFC. On the 26th, JG I moved up from Awoingt to the abandoned British airstrip at Léchelle.

Visiting Boistrancourt aerodrome on 17 March in Dr I 525/17, Rittm Manfred von Richthofen (left) confers with Jasta 5's commander, Oblt Richard Flashar, in preparation for the coming offensive. Ltn Hans-Joachim von Hippel is in the background at right. (Greg VanWyngarden)

Three of four Camels the Germans claimed on 27 March fell to Dr Is, including one to von Richthofen. 'With five machines of Jasta 11', he reported, 'I attacked at low height an English one-seater aeroplane and brought him down from a very close range with 150 bullets. The aeroplane fell into the flooded part of the Ancre'. Capt Thomas Sharpe of No. 73 Sqn RFC had scored six victories in the past two weeks, and was on a strafing mission when he was wounded and taken prisoner – even after the war he was convinced he had been brought down by ground fire. Another No. 73 Sqn RFC Camel was claimed by Kirschstein that afternoon.

Meanwhile, Ltn Heinrich Bongartz of Jasta 36 killed Lt H. W. Ransome of No. 70 Sqn RFC near Aveluy for his 33rd success. Elsewhere that same day, Jasta 6's triplanes attacked Armstrong-Whitworth FK 8 B5773 of No. 2 Sqn RFC south-west of Albert at 1520hrs. 2Lt Alan Arnett McLeod and Lt A. W. Hammond MC put up a spirited defence, claiming at least three of their assailants (although Jasta 6 recorded no casualties) until Ltn Kirschstein got in a decisive hit that set fire to the aeroplane's fuel tank. Even under those circumstances, 18-year-old McLeod from Stoneall, Manitoba, flew his 'Big Ack' while standing on the wing, with Hammond clung to the outside rim of his cockpit and continuing to blaze away with his Lewis gun.

The aeroplane finally crashed into a shell hole, where McLeod, though wounded four times, dragged Hammond – who had been wounded six times and was badly burned – into a shell hole just before the eight bombs attached to their FK 8 exploded, further injuring McLeod. He took a sixth bullet from German infantry before he and Hammond were rescued by British troops. McLeod was awarded the Victoria Cross (VC) for his extraordinary valour in that action.

Five minutes after making McLeod earn his VC, Kirschstein struck again, claiming a Camel north-east of Albert. This may well have been the aircraft of fellow Canadian 2Lt Alfred Koch of No. 70 Sqn (RFC), who survived the war with ten victories. He later described the punishment a Camel – or at least his Camel – could take:

It was in C8297 that I copped my second 'Blighty'. Despite 400 machine gun holes (not counting mine), this marvellous machine, with almost non-existent oil pressure from punctured oil tank for the concluding ten minutes of battle with four enemy aeroplanes and then a half-hour's flying from behind enemy lines back to my squadron, got me back home, where I was able to make a smooth quiet landing as if nothing had happened.

Such a smooth, dependable machine (if one survived the early weeks of overcoming torque of high degree) has rarely been built. And I say this as one of few, perhaps the only one, who has landed a Sopwith Camel upside down in a 30ft shell hole filled to within a foot of the top with water. We then had it apart the next day, with the wings hauled back from the second and third trench line area to the nearest roadway over which traffic could still move (over slippery duckboards) and the aircraft returned to the squadron, with only wing tips and leading edge damaged. I was flying over the lines in it again within three days!

It was No. 43 Sqn's turn to suffer on 28 March, with two pilots killed and three taken prisoner. Among the latter was 19-year-old Capt John Lightfoot Trollope, whose

18 victories included six in one day on 24 March. After burning a balloon and downing two Albatros D Vs on the 28th, Trollope was brought down wounded by Albatros pilot Ltn Paul Billik of Jasta 52 and his left hand had to be amputated. Climbing to aid his flight leader, 2Lt Cecil F King drew off two D Vs and claimed one, only to be wounded by a Dr I. Although credited to Ltn Werner of Jasta 14, King made it home, was promoted directly to captain and, in spite of his wounds, assumed leadership of Trollope's flight.

The fate of another No. 43 Sqn RFC man, 2Lt C. R. Maasdorp, was described by ace Ltn Ernst Udet, who spotted his Camel approaching at 150 metres:

At 80 metres he opens fire. It is impossible to avoid him, so I go straight for him. 'Tack, Tack, Tack' bellows mine at him, 'Tack, Tack, Tack' bellows his back at me.

We are still 20 metres apart, and it looks as though we will ram each other in another second. Then, a small movement, and he barely skims over me. His propwash shakes me, and the smell of castor oil flows past me.

I make a slight turn. 'Now begins the dogfight', I think. But he has also turned, and again we come at each other, firing like two tournament knights with lances at rest. This time I fly over him.

Another bank. Again, he is straight across from me, and once more we go for each other. The thin, white trails of the tracers hang in the air like curtains. He skims over me with barely a hand's width to spare – '8224' it says on his fuselage in black numerals.

The fourth time, I can feel my hands getting damp. That fellow there is a man who is fighting the fight of his life. Him or me – one has to go. There is no other way. For

A sober, spent Ltn Ernst Udet faces the camera upon landing following his gruelling aerial duel with 2Lt C. R. Maasdorp of No. 43 Sqn RFC on 28 March 1918. (Greg VanWyngarden)

the fifth time! The nerves are taut to bursting point, but the brain works coldly and clearly. This time the decision must fall. I line him up in my sights and go for him. I am resolved not to give an inch. We come at each other like mad boars. If he keeps his nerve, we will both be lost! Then he turns to avoid me.

At this moment he is caught by my burst. His aircraft rears, turns on its back and disappears in a gigantic crater. A fountain of earth, smoke. Twice I circle around the impact area. Field grey shapes are standing below, waving at me, shouting.

Udet visited a nearby field hospital to inquire about his late adversary:

The pilot had received a head shot and died instantaneously. The doctor handed me his wallet. Calling cards – 'Lieutenant Maasdorp, Ontario RFC 47'. A picture of an old woman and a letter. 'You mustn't fly so many sorties. Think of your father and me'.

A medic brought me the number of the aircraft. He had cut it out, and it was covered with a fine spray of blood flecks. I drove back to the Staffel. One must not think about that fact that a mother will cry for every man one brings down.

On 1 April the RFC and RNAS were amalgamated into the Royal Air Force, but most airmen on the Western Front were too busy to notice. JG 1 flew 106 sorties and claimed five victories that day, but the only Camel credited to one of its pilots fell to a Pfalz flown by Ltn Eugen Siempelkamp of Jasta 4. 2Lt P. R. Cann of No. 65 Sqn RAF was taken POW, but died of his wounds the next day.

Ltn Hans Weiss of Jasta 11 with his Dr I 545/17, as it probably looked during the historically momentous dogfights of 20–21 April 1918. He may have applied his namesake colour more extensively over the aeroplane by the time of his death on 2 May 1918. (Greg VanWyngarden)

Two days later Capt King of No. 43 Sqn RAF, still smarting from his wound and the loss of Capt Trollope, was leading Lt L. G. Loudon and Capt T. O'Neill on patrol when he spotted two triplanes over Morlancout at 0920hrs. The Camels promptly attacked and claimed one destroyed, which was credited to all three pilots, although the Germans recorded no Dr I casualties. The trio was jumped by four Albatroses soon after, but King and his men managed to fight their way clear and home. All three Camels had been badly shot about, but their pilots were miraculously none the worse for wear.

By 5 April Operation *Michael* had stalled near Amiens and was cancelled. With British forces drawn to that sector, the Germans launched a new push, called Operation *Georgette*, near Lys on the 9th. Progress was initially good, with Portuguese forces overrun, along with most of Messines Ridge and Armentières surrounded.

Meanwhile, the only lulls in aerial activity were dictated by the weather. The British lost 12 Camels on 6 April, eight of them to JG I. Early that afternoon No. 43 Sqn RAF was about to strafe German troops near Abancourt when it encountered a number of triplanes. Lt Hector C. Daniel claimed one in flames and 2Lt George A. Lingham reported killing the pilot of a Dr I that overshot him, but 2Lt H. S. Lewis, after having driven one down to crash, was killed by Udet near Hamel.

A follow-up patrol by No. 43 Sqn RAF fared worse, with three of six Camels falling to Ltn Hans Weiss, Ltn Erich Just and Vzfw Scholtz of Jasta 11. Capt King led his flight into another six triplanes and claimed one destroyed in a head-on attack. After sending an Albatros crashing, Lt Charles C. Banks had his petrol tanks holed and elevator cables shot away by ground fire, but he crash-landed in Allied lines. JG I recorded no losses, but a final Camel claim by Weiss at 1750hrs suggests that he, like King, may have perceived his opponent to be in more trouble than he really was.

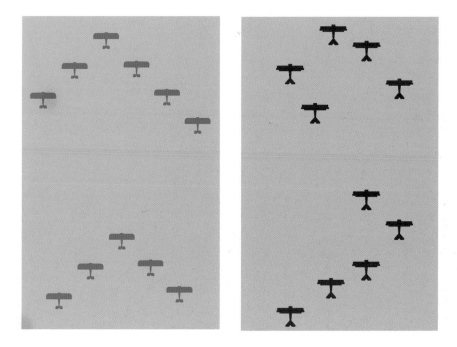

Typically, most Camel and Fokker Dr I units that clashed during the *Kaiserschlact* offensive were flying in formations identical to these seen here. RFC/RAF units split their aircraft up into flights of five or six aircraft (left), while the German Jastas favoured Kettes of four or five Dr Is (right).

In addition to Jasta 11's claims that day, Kirschstein of Jasta 6 brought 2Lt D. G. Gold of No. 3 Sqn RAF down as a POW north of Warfusée. Twenty minutes later von Richthofen reported:

> With five aeroplanes of Staffel 11, we attacked enemy single-seaters at low altitude flying near Villers Bretonneux. The British aircraft I attacked began to burn after only a few shots from my gun. Then it crashed burning to the ground in the small woods northeast of Villers Bretonneux, where it continued to burn.

His victim was Capt Sydney Philip Smith, a five-victory ace of No. 46 Sqn RAF.

On 7 April it was again No. 73 Sqn's turn to duel with JG I as the two units clashed over Villers Bretonneux at 1130hrs. 'We were told that the famous von Richthofen "Circus" was expected to be in the sky over the German lines at midday, and that our object was the give the "Circus" the biggest dusting possible', recalled Ronald Adam, then known as Lt Roland G. H. Adams. 'The plan called for us to fly at 17,000ft, and an SE 5 screen would cover us at 19,000ft'.

Von Richthofen, leading Jasta 11 and Jasta 6, spotted the SE 5as over Hangard and hit them first, probably sending 2Lt Philip J. Nolan of No. 24 Sqn RAF spiralling down to his death. Half-an-hour later it was No.73 Sqn's turn, and in a general melée in which both 2Lt R. R. Rowe and his newly-appointed flight leader, Capt Geoffrey A. H. Pidcock, claimed triplanes 'out of control', 2Lt Owen M. Baldwin singled out one and fired into it at 30yds, after which it spun down to crash near Cerisy. Baldwin's victim – the first of an eventual 16 that would make him No. 73 Sqn's top scorer – was probably Ltn Siegfried Gussmann of Jasta 11, who was slightly wounded.

Adams, meanwhile, was having trouble with his fuel system, and had to use his hand pump to keep the engine running while fighting for his life. Perhaps inevitably he found a triplane on his tail and was shot down, crashing into the railway line at the intersection of the old Roman Road and the road from Proyart to Harbonnières, where he was taken prisoner. That evening, an orderly informed him, 'Freiherr von Richthofen's compliments. You are his 78th victim'.

Jasta 11's Dr Is occupy Léchelle airfield in late March or early April 1918 – evidently with little time to alter their crosses to the more easily identifiable straight ones as prescribed by Idflieg on 17 March. (Greg VanWyngarden)

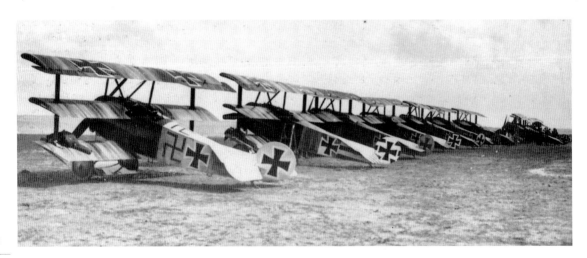

Maj Gilbert W. Murlis-Green, commander of No. 44 Sqn RFC, brings Sopwith Comic B5192 – a nightfighter version of the Camel, with twin overwing Lewis guns in place of the Vickers – in for a landing at Hainault Farm, in Essex. The Zeppelin-shaped wind vane on the hangar serves as a reminder of the home defence unit's purpose. Murlis-Green, formerly an ace with No. 17 Sqn in Salonika, brought down a Gotha G III on the night of 18 December 1917 for his eighth victory. (Greg VanWyngarden)

It is more likely that Adams was yet another victim of Ltn Kirschstein of Jasta 6, who claimed to have shot down a Camel at Proyart. Von Richthofen's account states:

I observed that a *Kette* flight of German aeroplanes pursuing a British aeroplane was being attacked from the rear. I dashed to their aid and attacked a British aeroplane. After I got behind him several times, the adversary fell. The aeroplane smashed into the ground and I saw that it crashed to splinters. This occurred 500 metres east of Hill 104.

Von Richthofen claimed a SPAD, but it seems that he misidentified both his opponent's aeroplane and its direction of descent. Most likely his 78th victim was 2Lt A. V. Gallie, whose Camel crashed west of Villers Brettoneux – the pilot returned to British lines uninjured.

Meanwhile, rain on 8 April had provided the Red Baron's Circus with an ideal occasion to take to the road again, first moving to Harbonnières and then to a grassy field along the road to Bray, one kilometre south of Cappy. Barracks were brought up from Rosières and erected, while British POWs joined a German machine gun company in preparing the take-off area. Captured British tents provided shelter to personnel and aircraft alike.

On 12 April Field Marshal Sir Douglas Haig sent the following message to his beleaguered army. 'With our backs to the wall, and believing in the justice of our cause, each one of us must fight on to the end'. His troops responded, and Allied counter-attacks on the 29th led to *Georgette*'s termination.

Whether or not it was inspired to any greater degree by Haig's 'backs to the wall' appeal, No. 43 Sqn RAF claimed 14 victories on the 12th for its most successful day of the war. Six of these successes (five Albatroses and a two-seater) were credited to Henry Woollett, giving the 'Fighting Cocks' the unique distinction of producing the only two British pilots to be credited with six victories in a day.

The Germans claimed five Camels on 12 April, but none fell victim to triplanes – credit for JG I's only Camel went to Ltn Erich Löwenhardt of Jasta 10. Camels do not

NEXT PAGE:
On 28 March 1918, No. 43 Sqn lost two pilots killed and three taken prisoner, the latter including Capt John L. Trollope, whose 18 victories included six in one day before he was brought down wounded by Albatros pilot Ltn Paul Billik of Jasta 52. Whilst climbing to aid his flight leader (Trollope), 2Lt Cecil F. King in Camel D1777 drew two Albatros D Vs toward him and claimed one – possibly Ltn Hans-Georg von der Osten of Jasta 4, who came down wounded. As this battlescene reveals, King was then jumped himself and wounded by a Fokker Dr I that was almost certainly being flown by ace Ltn Hans Werner of Jasta 14 (shown here in his Dr I 198/17). In spite of his injuries, the Camel pilot struggled back home, and subsequently assumed leadership of Trollope's flight. Surviving the war with 22 victories to his credit, King was killed in a flying accident on 24 January 1919.

Mark Postlethwaite - 01

seem to have been responsible for JG I's casualties of the 12th either, with the Jagdgeschwader having Uffz Robert Eiserbeck of Jasta 11 killed near Méault at 1510hrs and Ltn Wolff of Jasta 6 slightly wounded.

Aside from the latter pilot being more severely wounded on the 19th, necessitating his being evacuated to hospital, the next confrontation between Camel and Dr I would not occur until 20 April. The dogfights that would follow more or less marked the climax of JG I's triplane activity, and sealed the legendary status of the triplane and Camel alike, for they encompassed the last 24 hours of Manfred von Richthofen's life.

The first encounter began in the afternoon of 20 April amid the first clear flying weather JG I had enjoyed in four days. Leading six triplanes of Jasta 11 in his all-red Dr I 425/17, von Richthofen spotted what he described as 'a large *Geschwader*' of Camels south-west of Bois de Hamel at 1840hrs.

The Baron's opponents, actually 11 Camels of No. 3 Sqn RAF, now based at Valheureux, had also been grounded by bad weather until 1700hrs, when two flights departed on an offensive patrol. Somewhat unusually, 'C' Flight, composed of Capt D. J. Bell, Lt G. R. Riley, 1Lt L. A. Hamilton, Lt Squires and 2Lt D. G. Lewis, was being led by the squadron commander, Maj Richard Raymond-Barker MC, who in spite of the six victories he had scored in Bristol F 2Bs the year before, now spent more time dealing with administrative duties than he did combat flying. Behind it, 'A' Flight's Capt Leman led 2Lts Boyd, McElroy, McIntyre and Kinney. The latter pilot recalled:

Our two flights lost contact because we took off at different intervals and because of the still squally weather. The entire front was overhung with low, dark clouds, but Capt Leman, undisturbed by the separation, kept a straight course. We eventually found 'C' Flight after about an hour, scrambled up in a widespread dogfight and outnumbered by a large group of brightly coloured Fokker triplanes.

A line-up of Jasta 12 Dr Is dominates Le Mesnil aerodrome in June 1918. By that time JG II's triplanes were more likely to encounter French SPADs than Camels, and the summer heat was raising havoc with the ersatz castor oil that lubricated the Oberursel engines fitted to the Dr Is of Jastas 12 and 19. (Greg VanWyngarden)

Von Richthofen had by then already drawn first blood, as he noted. 'During the fight I observed that a triplane was attacked and shot at from below by a Camel. I positioned myself behind the adversary and brought him down, burning, with only a few shots. The aeroplane crashed near Hamel Wood, where it burned on the ground'. His victim, Maj Raymond-Barker, was killed. Kinney continues:

As we approached, directly in front of me a Camel turned on its side and plummeted to the earth, leaving a trail of thick black smoke. I couldn't take my eyes off the terrible sight. What a ghastly way to die, burned to death in the sky! If any pain-wracked life remained during the plunge, it ended on violent impact with the earth. I only had time to think 'the poor devil ... not a chance in the world' then I was in the midst of it.

I suddenly saw the flash of a bright red triplane looming before me – the most terrifying thing I had seen in the air. I wanted to turn west and scram, but something wouldn't let me. Instead, I pointed my nose at the red devil and pressed my Vickers gun controls. Both machine guns opened up and I saw my tracers going toward the fuselage of the red fighter. At the same moment I heard a distinct 'pop-pop-pop' right behind me, and thin blue threads of tracer bullets passed through my wing planes much too close for comfort. I risked a quick glance backward and saw a green and white triplane veering in on me.

To save myself from becoming another fiery furnace like the one I had just seen, I jammed on right rudder and pushed the control stick forward and right to make myself an impossible target. My Camel responded beautifully by immediately snapping into a spin with engine full on. I held her there for a few seconds and then straightened out. When I looked around, there wasn't an aeroplane to be seen in the sky. Like most dogfights, it had been a quick encounter, in for the kill and out.

Kinney had witnessed von Richthofen shoot down No. 3 Sqn's youngest member, 'Tommy' Lewis. The Red Baron reported:

This side view of Sopwith Camel N6332 shows the concentration of weight and power up front, which contributed to the new fighter's dazzling manoeuvrability. Indeed, it was only the Camel's agility that saved American pilot 2Lt M. Curtis Kinney of No. 3 Sqn RAF on the afternoon of 20 April 1918, when he fought against von Richthofen's 'Circus'. (Museum of Flight Peter Bowers Collection)

Three minutes after I had shot down the first one in flames, I attacked a second Camel from this same Geschwader. The opponent went into a dive, pulled out and repeated this manoeuvre several times. As he did that, I came up to the closest fighting distance and fired about 50 rounds at him until his machine caught fire. The fuselage burned in the air and the rest of the aeroplane crashed northeast of Villers Brettonneux.

Remarkably, although his blazing descent burned away his fuselage and tail fabric, Lewis managed enough control to crash-land, and after being thrown through the upper wing, got to his feet with minor burns. The Rhodesian teenager was taken prisoner, but he had every reason to feel grateful just to be able to tell his grandchildren how he survived his run-in with the Red Baron.

Lloyd Hamilton, a New Yorker in the USAS temporarily attached to No. 3 Sqn, was at the tail-end of 'C' Flight when he saw Lewis go down. Moments later he engaged a blue Dr I. Closing to 100yds and firing 300 rounds, he saw it dive and then go into a spin. Hamilton fired a few more rounds and then pulled up to discover no further aircraft in sight. He claimed a triplane driven down, but it was not confirmed.

Jasta 11 claimed a third victory in the fight. Kinney's description of being attacked by a 'green and white triplane' suggests that he may have been credited as Ltn Weiss's 15th victory, since Weiss painted the upper wing and most of the fuselage and tail surfaces of his Dr I 545/17 white ('Weiss' in German). Another possibility, however,

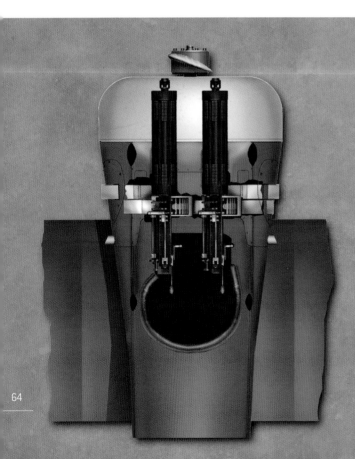

SOPWITH F 1 CAMEL FUSELAGE GUNS

The Camel was the first Sopwith design to feature two 0.303-in. Vickers machine guns. The weapons fired through the propeller thanks to either the Constantinesco C C synchronizing mechanism (fitted to 100hp Le Rhône Camels) or the Kauper No. 3 interruptor gear (used by 130hp Clerget-powered Camels).

was 'Jack' Riley, who was wounded but managed to return. Back at Valheureux, 'Ginger' Bell was credited with a triplane destroyed, although in fact all of von Richthofen's 'gentlemen' had returned safely to Cappy.

After the two sides disengaged, Wolff wrote that von Richthofen 'went down very low so that everyone could recognize his red machine', and he was greeted by waves and hats flung in the air from appreciative German infantrymen. 'After *Herr Rittm* landed', Wolff continued, 'he smacked his hands together as he said, "*Donnerwetter*! Eighty is a respectable number!" And we were all happy for him, and thrilled about his success'. Von Richthofen was undoubtedly setting his sights on an even rounder number, 100, an ambition that might be all the more attainable when the Fokker D VIIs arrived.

Heavy fog grounded JG I at Cappy throughout Sunday morning, 21 April. While his pilots marked time in various ways, the Geschwader Adjutant, Oblt Karl Bodenschatz – not for the first time – broached the matter of von Richthofen's retiring from his combat role and applying his wealth of experience as an inspector of German fighter aviation.

Aside from the influence he could have on expediting the development and deployment of better fighters for the Jagdstaffeln, the German high command realized the propaganda value the reigning – and living – ace of aces had for the entire war effort. Von Richthofen, however, dismissed the suggestion out of hand. 'A paper-shuffler? No! I am staying at the Front!'

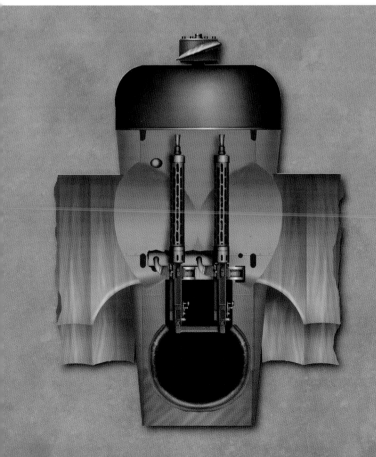

FOKKER Dr I FUSELAGE GUNS

The Dr I was armed with two tried and tested 7.92mm LMG 08/15 machine guns, synchronized using Fokker's *Zentralsteurung* interruptor gear. The Dr I could carry 1,000 rounds of ammunition.

Three flights of Camels from No. 209 Sqn engaged the Red Baron on his final, fateful, mission on the morning of 21 April 1918, with the second flight of five Sopwith fighters being led by ace Lt Oliver W. 'Noll' Redgate. Subsequently credited with sending a Dr I down out of control on 2 May 1918 (for his 15th victory), Redgate was wounded in the leg dogfighting with another triplane 13 days later. Despite the seriousness of his injuries, he survived the war with 16 victories to his name. (Denny May)

So the matter rested until a strong east wind dissipated the ground mist and a telephoned report came in at 1030hrs that British aircraft were approaching the lines. Within minutes two Ketten of Jasta 11 Dr Is were taking off to deal with them. The first, led by von Richthofen, included his newly arrived cousin, Ltn Wolfram von Richthofen, as well as Oblt Walther Karjus, Scholtz and Wolff. Weiss again led the second.

At 0935hrs the first of 15 Camels of No. 209 Sqn RAF had left Bertangles, Capt Roy Brown leading four, followed by Lt Oliver W. Redgate's five-aeroplane flight and Capt Oliver C. Le Boutillier's five Camels. At 1025hrs Le Boutillier's flight engaged two Albatros two-seaters 12,000ft over Le Quesnel, and Le Boutillier, with Lts Robert M. Foster and Merrill Samuel Taylor, sent one down in flames. Twenty minutes later No. 209 Sqn RAF reported encountering 'a large formation of Fokker triplanes and Albatros D Vs', and the main event was on. Wolff subsequently described this fateful engagement in a letter to the convalescing Lothar von Richthofen:

Scarcely had we arrived at the front when from this side and below us, in the area around Hamel, we saw about seven Sopwith Camels. In addition to the five of us, Jasta 5 (Albatros D Vs) was still in the vicinity, but much farther away near Sailly le Sec. Above us were seven more Camels, some of which attacked Jasta 5 and some of which remained above.

One or two came at us. We began to fight. In the course of the fight I saw that *Herr Rittm* was often near me, but he had not yet shot at anything. Of our *Kette*, only Oblt Karjus was next to me. Vzfw Scholtz was fighting in the vicinity of Sailly le Sec, along with the Albatroses. Ltn Wolfram von Richthofen was apparently not yet completely ready, as this was perhaps his first aerial combat.

While Oblt Karjus and I fought against two or three Camels, suddenly I saw the red machine near me, as he fired at a Camel that first went into a spin, then slipped away in a steep dive toward the west. This fight took place on the other side over the heights of Hamelet.

We had a rather strong east wind, and *Herr Rittm* had not taken that into account. As I now had clear air around me, I got closer to a Camel and shot it down. As the Camel went down, I looked over at *Herr Rittm* and saw that he was at extremely low altitude over the Somme near Corbie, right behind an Englishman. I shook my head instinctively and wondered why *Herr Rittm* was following an opponent so far on the other side.

While I was looking to see where my opponent had fallen, suddenly I heard a machine gun behind me and I was being attacked by another Camel, which had already put 20 holes in my machine. When I luckily got free of that one, I looked around for *Herr Rittm*, but saw no one else except Oblt Karjus, who was close to me, but also not yet completely ready for combat. Then I became a bit uneasy, as I certainly should have seen *Herr Rittm*. We circled the area for a time, and again were attacked by an Englishman who followed us up to about 900 metres over Corbie – but of *Herr Rittm* there was no trace.

Wolff was credited with the Camel, but his victim, Lt William F. Mackenzie, returned to base wounded. He in turn may have been a 'triplane with a blue tail' that Lt Francis J. W. Mellersh was credited with driving 'down in a vertical dive to crash near Cerisy'.

Meanwhile, two new, inexperienced pilots who had been told to stay above any fighting encountered one another, and 2Lt Wilfrid R. 'Wop' May attacked Wolfram von Richthofen. The latter dove away, with May in pursuit, right through the swirling dogfight. May, in classic beginner's style, sustained his fire too long, resulting in both guns jamming, so he spun down and headed west into the sun. Soon after levelling off, he found himself being fired on from behind. May wrote later:

Whichever bullet killed Manfred von Richthofen, it was 2Lt Wilfrid Reid May's lucky failure to go down that was primarily responsible for the target fixation that led the Red Baron to his doom on 21 April 1918. 'Wop' May would later help bring down fellow 'Circus' member Ltn Fedor Hubner of Jasta 4 as a POW in Dr I 546/17 on 16 May. (Denny May)

I noticed it was a red triplane, but if I realised it was von Richthofen, I would have probably passed out on the spot. I kept on dodging and spinning, I imagine from about 12,000ft, until I ran out of sky and had to hedge hop over the ground. Von Richthofen was firing at me continually, and the only thing that saved me was my poor flying. I didn't know what I was doing myself, and I do not suppose that von Richthofen could figure out what I was going to do.

Weiss's Kette was also attacked by seven red-nosed Camels, which one of its members, Ltn Richard Wenzl, called the 'anti-Richthofen people'. He also recalled:

We went through the paces, but due to the strong east wind, we drifted farther and farther over the other side. Accordingly, Weiss broke off combat and headed back over the lines. With that, suddenly I saw that one of our machines was in trouble. Afterwards, someone told me that he was sure it was *Wölffchen* (Hans-Joachim Wolff). In the air I thought I had recognised von Richthofen's machine. One after another, the other machines came back. We landed and everyone was there – only von Richthofen was missing.

'Wop' May continued his account of the fight:

We came over the German lines and troops fired at us as we went over – this was also the case coming over the British lines. I got on the Somme River and started up the valley at a very low altitude. Von Richthofen was very close on my tail. I went around a curve in the river just near Corbie, but von Richthofen beat me to it and came over the hill. At that point I was a sitting duck, as I was too low down between the banks to make a turn away from him.

At that point May, certain he was doomed, looked back 'and saw von Richthofen do a spin-and-a-half and hit the ground. I looked up and saw one of our machines directly behind. I joined up with him and returned to our aerodrome'.

While von Richthofen had been pursuing May, he in turn had been followed by Roy Brown, who had fired bursts at him from long range. The red triplane was also being fired at by the 53rd Australian Field Battery and the 24th Machine gun Company.

Given the jinking about that both aeroplanes did throughout the chase, the single bullet that mortally wounded von Richthofen could have come from Brown – who was credited with the victory – or any of the Aussies. What indisputably ended the Red Baron's career, however, was his ego-driven failure, in his obsession to finish the uncooperative 'Wop' May, to heed an essential point in his own *Air Combat Operations Manual*:

One should never obstinately stay with an opponent which, through bad shooting or skilful turning, he had been unable to shoot down when the battle lasts until it is on the other side, and one alone is faced by a greater number of opponents.

ENGAGING THE ENEMY

The most common gunsighting system seen in fighters on both sides by 1918 was the ring and bead arrangement. The ring, made of steel strip of about 3in. diameter, with four radial wires attached to an inner ring of 0.5in., 1in. in diameter, allowed for the speed and direction of a moving target, as well as that of the pilot's own aeroplane. With experience, airmen learned to fire at aircraft appearing at the outer edges of the ring, rather than when they were lined up with the inner ring and bead on a pylon mounted forward of the ring. Unless a fighter lay dead ahead or astern of its opponent, the target was unlikely to still be in the centre of the inner ring by the time the pilot's bullets reached it.

A more sophisticated variant on the ring and bead were the tubular British Aldis or German Oigee sights, which contained hermetically-sealed collimating lenses and an inert gas to prevent fogging in varying weather conditions. Oigee also developed an early type of reflector sight, but the handful of examples produced were only mounted on a few Albatros D Vs and Fokker Dr Is of Jasta 12 for frontline evaluation – they never saw widespread use. Aldis sights appeared frequently on Sopwith Camels and SE 5as, but Oigee sights were more the exception than the rule on German fighters.

Whatever the tactical dicta had to say about aiming and bringing down an enemy aircraft, in practice there was no substitute for catching one's opponent unawares. In the wildly turning dogfights between Camel and Dr I, a pilot simply had to be ready to get his shot off at a target of opportunity, for which the ring and bead sight was better suited. The ring and bead allowed the option of focusing, or allowing one's peripheral vision to take in the scene around him, whereas pilots were more prone to becoming target fixated when peering through an Aldis type sight, and this could prove fatal. The artwork seen here reveals a pursuing pilot in about as favourable a position as he could get when chasing an opponent – in this case a skilled triplane pilot on the tail of a jinking Camel.

When DH 4s of No. 5 Sqn RNAS made an escorted bombing attack on Busigny aerodrome on 18 March 1918, it was intended to provoke a German response, but this time the British got more than they had bargained for in the form of 50 fighters from Jastas 3, 4, 5, 6, 10, 11, 16b, 34b, 37, 46, 54 and 56.

Although the British claimed nine victories, the Germans only noted the loss of four aeroplanes and three pilots, while downing 13 aircraft, eight of them Camels. Amongst the five Camels lost by No. 54 Sqn RFC was the aircraft flown by unit CO, Capt F. L. Luxmoore, who came under attack by Ltn Hans Kirschstein of Jasta 6, as seen here in this artwork.

Once a pilot got on the tail of his opponent, it became primarily a matter of staying behind and above the target, firing measured machine gun bursts whenever it appeared at the right position on the sight ring, until a bullet hit the pilot, engine or another vital component. In this case, Luxmoore's engine was hit by one of Kirschstein's bursts and he force-landed, surviving as a POW.

Von Richthofen's loss sent a shock wave through the Luftstreitskräfte, but the British lost at least one Camel to Dr Is that day too – Lt C. J. Mason of No. 54 Sqn RAF, killed west of Bailleul by Ltn Karl Gallwitz of Jasta Boelcke.

On 22 April the British buried von Richthofen with full military honours near Bertangles. Back at Cappy, Oblt Bodenschatz opened the Red Baron's official testament and found its sole purpose was to name his Hptm Wilhelm Reinhard as his successor to command JG I. The next day Jasta 11 patrolled the same area, and Weiss and Wolff had the vindictive satisfaction of downing two Camels north of Moreuil, killing Capt G. A. Magor and 2Lt W. H. Easty of No. 201 Sqn RAF.

Operation *Georgette* may have ended on 29 April, but all remained far from quiet over the Western Front. On 2 May Jasta 11 lost two more aces when Ltn Weiss, whose score stood at 16, was shot down by 'Sammy' Taylor of No. 209 Sqn RAF, and Vzfw Scholtz, then credited with six victories, and looking forward to receiving his leutnant's commission, fatally crashed during a take-off attempt later in the day. In a letter to a lady friend of Taylor's, Capt 'Noll' Redgate, who had also claimed a triplane, described Weiss' demise:

> We came across the Hun Circus – this was after the Baron was shot down – and, of course, we attacked them. There was one pilot which showed himself to be a wonderful fighter, and his machine was painted all white. We all had a shot at him, but Sam stuck to him and it was a case of the better man lives. After a long fight Sam eventually got him clean, and down he went.

Apart from the controversies of 21 April, in May No. 209 Sqn RAF seemed to come as close as any British fighter unit to earning the 'anti-Richthofen' monicker Wenzl had given it. On the 9th Le Boutillier was credited with a triplane that crashed south of Bray. Its pilot, Ltn Johann Janzen, commander of Jasta 6, suffered a severed rudder cable, but was blown east by the wind into marshland near the Somme and emerged unhurt. Janzen himself stated that he was downed in a scrap with SE 5as, but curiously no SE 5a pilot claimed a triplane that day.

On 16 May Sam Taylor, Capt Stearne T. Edwards and 'Wop' May brought Ltn Fedor Hubner of Jasta 4 down in Dr I 546/17 – the German pilot became a POW. At 1620hrs that same day, Capt James H. Forman of No. 201 Sqn RAF claimed a triplane in flames south of Albert that matched the death of Jasta 4's Sgt Otto Schmutzler near Proyart at 2000hrs.

On 18 May Wenzl flew to 2. Armee Flug Park to exchange his Dr I for a new Fokker D VII fitted with a 160hp Mercedes engine. Besides the superior speed and overall high-altitude performance the latter machine offered its pilot, Wenzl recalled everyone being pleased to be returning to stationary, water-cooled engines. 'The inferior Rizinus oil, the elixir of life for rotary engines, made it so apparent that on hot days there would be no end to the forced landings'.

By the end of May 1918, D VIIs were mainstays at Jastas 6, 10 and 11, while Jasta 4 operated Jasta 6's and 11's castoff Dr Is until enough D VIIs could replace those as well.

STATISTICS AND ANALYSIS

An attempt to evaluate the aerial duels between the Camel and the Fokker Dr I is handicapped by the fact that they were not fought in an *in vitro* environment, but in an untidy sky filled with other formidable adversaries on both sides. That said, statistics may be derived from known Dr I pilots' claims over Camels, and vice versa, in the course of those encounters they did have during the *Kaiserschlacht*.

A check of claims by British aces over Fokker triplanes throughout the war yields some remarkable totals. While Camel aces were credited with 87 of them, 94 were credited to SE 5a pilots, 67 to Bristol Fighter crews, 14 to Sopwith Dolphin aces, three to DH 4 crews and one Dr I 'out of control' to a Nieuport 27 flown by Canadian Capt Earl S. Meek of No. 29 Sqn RFC for his fifth of six victories on 28 January 1918. The total of such claims, 266, falls just 54 short of all the Fokker triplanes ever produced!

Narrowing the focus to the Camel versus the Dr I in the period between the beginning of March and the end of May 1918, when triplane activity was at its peak, Dr I units claimed a total of 56 Camels. Actual Camel combat casualties during those three months totalled 32, with 19 pilots killed, eight taken POW and five wounded. Camel claims over triplanes in that time period came to 61, compared to 13 admitted German casualties – four pilots killed, four POWs and five wounded.

As previously noted, a good many claims on both sides may be explained by the occasionally documented cases of airmen force-landing unhurt, with the Germans benefiting from doing so on their side of the lines more often than their British counterparts. Others, as also seen in some instances, were simple cases of multi-claiming or overclaiming in good faith due to misconceptions in the heat of combat.

A highly successful Camel ace, Capt John L Trollope claimed 18 victories, including six in one day on 24 March 1918. However, only a fraction of these claims can be borne out by actual German losses. The same can be said for the 1,294 victories credited to Camel pilots overall. Trollope did not claim a single Dr I victory. (Jon Guttman)

The British were especially prone to doing this throughout the war, but in spite of their supposedly strict confirmation standards, and the advantage of usually having the evidence either behind or within sight of their lines, it is remarkable how often German pilots got away with spurious claims.

The earliest case in point occurred on 3 February 1918, when Flt Cdr R. R. Winter was credited with a triplane for which there was no corresponding recorded German loss, while Jasta 26 was credited with no fewer than five Camels shot down, in spite of Winter being the only British loss for the entire day!

Within the available statistics, one might also examine how the quality of the victims reflects that of the opposing airmen, which amid Germany's recorded casualties represents an extraordinarily high percentage of paladins. Dr I losses to Camels during this period included the injured Lothar von Richthofen, who would return to combat four months later and raise his score to 40, before being wounded again on 13 August 1918. Fellow ace Hans Weiss, with 16 victories, was also killed in action, while Ltn Siegfried Gussmann had four victories to his credit when wounded on 7 April 1918 (probably by 2Lt Owen M. Baldwin of No. 73 Sqn RAF). He eventually returned to flying and scored a fifth victory to become an ace.

The most celebrated victim of them all, of course, was Manfred von Richthofen with 80. Crediting his demise to Roy Brown is fraught with danger, however, as there is a wealth of evidence favouring Australian ground fire as the more likely cause of the Red Baron's death.

Among those Dr I pilots known to have either crash-landed or at least given a plausible impression of being in trouble after an engagement with Camels were Johann Janzen (13 victories) and Josef Jacobs (48). Eberhardt Mohnicke (nine victories) and Erich Just (six) of Jasta 11 were wounded on 1 March 1918, but it is uncertain as to whether their opponents were Camels of No. 54 Sqn RFC or fighters from one of the other four units that claimed out of control victories that day.

The list of Camel casualties at the hands of Dr Is between March and May 1918 was by no means confined to hapless tyros. Three aces have been included among the eight Camels claimed by the Red Baron – Thomas S. Sharpe of No. 73 Sqn RFC, who had six victories by the time he became a POW on 27 March 1918; Sydney Philip Smith of No. 46 Sqn RAF, who had claimed five victories prior to being killed on 6 April; and Maj Richard Raymond-Barker of No. 3 Sqn RAF, who had six to his credit (previously scored in Bristol F 2Bs) prior to becoming victim No. 79 on 20 April.

Wounded in the latter action, possibly by Hans Weiss, was George R. Riley, who had four victories at the time, and subsequently went on to total 13. Also among the wounded Camel aces was Cecil King of No. 43 Sqn RFC, who claimed an

Albatros D V for his eighth success – possibly putting Ltn Hans-Georg von der Osten, a five-victory ace, and commander of Jasta 4, out of the war with serious wounds – just before being hit on 28 March. Although credited to Ltn Hans Werner of Jasta 14, King made it back to Allied lines, and would finish the war with 22 victories.

Adding Kurt Wolff, killed in F I 102/17 on 15 September 1917, and Otto Esswein with 12 victories, possibly killed by Camels of No. 73 Sqn RAF west of Bois de Belleau on 21 July 1918, to the list of *Kaiserschlacht* casualties provides a reasonably firm foundation for the Camel's reputation as an ace-killer.

But was its manoeuvrability any more decisive a factor than the hit-and-run capabilities of faster British fighters? An answer can be seen in the triplane aces who fell victim to other British aircraft during the *Kaiserschlacht*. On 17 March 1918 Ltn Steinhäuser was wounded in the foot, most likely by an SE 5a of No. 84 Sqn RFC, and forced to land at Jasta 3's aerodrome at Briastre.

On 29 April, Ltn Heinrich Bongartz of Jasta 36 (33 victories) was severely wounded by an SE 5a of No. 74 Sqn RAF. Four days later Ltn Just was wounded in the neck, probably by Capt Cyril N Lowe and Lt Ronald T. Mark of No. 24 Sqn RAF, although he would later return to combat and be credited with six victories. On 16 May Ltn Hans-Joachim Wolff (ten victories) was slain north of Lamotte Ferme by Capt Horace D Barton of No. 24 Sqn RAF. Prior to *Kaiserschlacht*, of course, Werner Voss famously died fighting No. 56 Sqn's SE 5as on 23 September 1917.

Augustus Orlebar of No. 73 Sqn RFC has had to share his claim over Lothar von Richthofen with the Bristol team of Geoffrey F. Hughes and Hugh Claye of No. 62 Sqn RFC. And even when the opposition was not a fighter of comparable performance, the best triplane pilot was not immune to the proverbial bullet with his

Ltn Johann Janzen, commander of Jasta 6, poses proudly before his Dr I 403/17. After surviving being shot down by 'Boots' LeBoutillier on 9 May 1918, Janzen stated that he had fallen victim to SE 5as, but no victories were claimed by pilots flying this type on that particular day. (Greg VanWyngarden)

name on it. Flying triplane 419/17 on 10 April 1918, Jasta 19's commander, Ltn Walter Göttsch, was credited with his 20th victory over an RE 8 of No. 52 Sqn RAF, but although wounded, its crew, 2Lts H. L. Taylor and W. I. E. Lane, hit the Dr I with a burst of fire that killed the ace.

Three days after becoming Staffelführer of Jasta 36 on 16 May 1918, Ltn Richard Plange, victor in seven combats, was killed by Lts W Hughes and F C Peacock, flying a lumbering Armstrong Whitworth FK 10 of No. 10 Sqn RAF. Whatever controversy remains regarding the Red Baron's demise, there is no argument that Ltn Hans von Haebler, who had scored eight victories with Jasta 36, was brought down by anti-aircraft fire over Bapaume on 22 March 1918, his Dr I 509/17 falling into British hands, while he died of his wounds the next day.

Lt Oliver Colin LeBoutillier shows off the unique set of white bands he had applied to his Camel D3338 while serving as a flight leader in No. 209 Sqn RAF. (Jon Guttman)

LEADING CAMEL Dr I KILLERS

Pilot	Squadron	Dr Is	Total
Capt William L. Jordan	208	5	36
Capt William S. Stephenson	73	4	11
Capt Owen M. Baldwin	73	3	16
Capt John Todd	70	3	18
Capt Douglas G. Bell	3	2	16
Capt Orlando C. Bridgeman	80	2	5
Maj Alfred W. Carter	210	2	17
Lt Hector C. Daniel	43	2	9
Capt James H. Forman	201	2	9
Lt Gavin L. Graham	73	2	13
Capt Cecil F. King	43	2	16
Capt Robert A. Little	203	2	47
Capt Norman MacMillan	45	2	9
Lt Wilfrid R. May	209	2	13
Capt Francis J. W. Mellersh	209	2	5
Capt Cyril B. Ridley	201	2	11
Lt Anthony G. A. Spence	1(N), 201	2	9
Lt Merrill S. Taylor	209	2	7
Capt Alfred Whistler	80	2	23

LEADING Dr I CAMEL KILLERS

Pilot	Jasta	Camels	Total
Rittm Manfred von Richthofen	JG I	8	80
Ltn Hans Kirschstein	6	6	26
Ltn Werner Voss	10	6	48
OffzSt Otto Esswein	26	4	12
Ltn Fritz Loerzer	26	4	11
Ltn Hans Weiss	11	4	16

A view of Ltn Lothar von Richthofen's badly damaged Dr I 454/17 after the combat of 13 March 1918. His aeroplane was claimed by both a Camel pilot of No. 73 Sqn RFC and a Bristol F 2B crew of No. 62 Sqn RFC. (Greg VanWyngarden)

AFTERMATH

Jasta 27 was late in
receiving its Dr Is, one of
which is shown here at the
unit's Halluin-Ost airfield
in May 1918. By then the
triplane's successor in the
form of a newly delivered
Fokker D VII, can already
be seen in the background.
(Greg VanWyngarden)

After peaking between March and May 1918, the clash between Sopwith Camel and
Fokker Dr I did not end in a decisive climax, but merely fizzled away as the D VII
replaced the triplane – a process accelerated as the summer heat made it harder to
keep the latter fighters' rotaries running. Even at their apex during the *Kaiserschlacht*,
the Dr Is may have seen action as the tip of the Luftstreitskräfte's spear, but they were
still too few in number to serve as more than the vanguard of local air superiority
without a substantial back-up from older types. Indeed, it was the Albatros D V which
equipped most German fighter units at the front at this time, along with a number
of Pfalz D IIIs.

Kaiserschlacht was not over, but its next phase, Operation *Blücher-Yorck* on 27 May, was aimed at French-held trenches and elements of the American Expeditionary Force between Soissons and Reims, followed by Operation *Gneisenau* on 9 June, which French counterattacks stopped at Compiègne two days later. With French and American aircraft now being the Germans' principal opposition, Camel-versus-triplane duels rapidly diminished. Moreover, during that time Fokker D VIIs became increasingly available to the Jagdgeschwader, and their Dr Is were handed down to other units such as Jastas 5 and 34b, or to *Jastaschulen* as trainers.

By the time of the last offensive along the Marne River on 15 July, most of the Dr Is had been grounded through overheating engines. Jastas 14 and 36 seem to have kept a few flying as late as August, and Jasta 59 had one left in September – probably flown by its commander, ex-Jasta 11 member Oblt Hans-Helmut von Boddien – until D VIIs became available to it at the end of the month.

The RAF's air war continued, with Camels soldiering on alongside SE 5as, Bristol F 2Bs and Sopwith Dolphins and Snipes, while their primary opponent, the Fokker D VII, was supplemented by Roland D VIs, Pfalz D XIIs and, for want of enough newer types, leftover Albatros D Vas and Pfalz D IIIas. There was also the odd diehard still engaging the enemy in the Dr I, most notably Ltn Josef Jacobs of Jasta 7, who kept two flying until October 1918, replacing their engines outright by offering a case of champagne to the ground troops for every workable rotary they recovered from downed enemy aeroplanes.

Although the Allied preponderance in numbers steadily grew, the 11 November armistice found the Jagdstaffeln in retreat, but still full of fight – and a great many of their airmen bitter about Germany's capitulation.

As far as overall impact on the war effort goes, the Camel would seem to win easily on the basis of sheer numbers, and time in service. It did not really drive the Fokker triplane from the sky, however. Rather, the Dr I was eclipsed by something better, not only from the same country, but from the same company.

Canadian Lt Floyd W. Wells stands beside his Camel of No.80 Sqn RAF – a unit that specialized in ground attack for most of the war – at Donstiennes, in Belgium, in December 1918. (Floyd W. Wells album via Jon Guttman)

FURTHER
READING

Beedle, J., *43 Squadron Royal Flying Corps, Royal Air Force – The History of the Fighting Cocks, 1916–66* (Beaumont Aviation Literature, London, 1966)

Bowyer, Chaz, *Sopwith Camel, King of Combat* (Glassney Press, Oxford, 1978)

Bruce, J. M., *The Fokker Dr I* (Profile Publications Ltd, Leatherhead, Surrey, 1965)

Bruce, J. M., *The Sopwith F 1 Camel* (Profile Publications Ltd., Leatherhead, Surrey, 1965)

Cook, Fulton, *Lieut Lloyd A Hamilton of the 17th Aero Squadron* (Cross & Cockade (USA) Journal, p.70, Vol.20, No.1, Winter 1979)

Franks, Norman and Frank Bailey, *Above the Lines* (Grub Street, London, 1993)

Franks, Norman, Frank Bailey and Gregory Alegi, *Above the War Fronts* (Grub Street, London, 1997)

Franks, Norman, Frank Bailey and Rick Duiven, *The Jasta War Chronology* (Grub Street, London, 1998)

Franks, Norman, Russell Guest and Frank Bailey, *Bloody April ... Black September* (Grub Street, London, 1995)

Franks, Norman and Greg VanWyngarden, *Osprey Aircraft of the Aces 40 – Fokker Dr I Aces of World War 1* (Osprey Publishing, Oxford, 2001)

Franks, Norman, *Osprey Aircraft of the Aces 52 – Sopwith Camel Aces of World War 1* (Osprey Publishing, Oxford, 2003)

Franks, Norman, *Osprey Aircraft of the Aces 78 – SE 5/5a Aces of World War 1* (Osprey Publishing, Oxford, 2007)

Fraser, Alan, *A Month With 4 Squadron Australian Flying Corps* (Cross & Cockade International Journal, p.7, Vol 23, No.1, Spring 1992)

Hadingham, Evan, *The Fighting Triplanes* (The Macmillan Company, New York, NY, 1968)

Imrie, Alex, *The Fokker Triplane* (Arms and Armour Press, London, 1992)

Kilduff, Peter, *Richthofen – Beyond the Legend of the Red Baron* (Arms & Armour Press, London, 1993)

Kinney, Lt Curtis, RAF with Dale Titler, *I Flew A Camel* (Dorrance and Company, Philadelphia, PA, 1972)

Lawson, Stephen T., *Jasta 7 Under Köbes* (Cross & Cockade International Journal, Vol.25, Nos 2 and 3, 1994)

Lee, Arthur Gould, *No Parachute – A Fighter Pilot in World War I* (Harper & Row, New York, NY, 1970)

Puglisi, William R., *Jacobs of Jasta 7* (Cross & Cockade (USA) Journal, p.334, Vol.6, No.4, Winter 1965)

Revell, Alex, *British Single-Seater Fighter Squadrons on the Western Front in World War I* (Schiffer Publishing Ltd, Atlgen, PA, 2006)

Shores, Christopher, Norman Franks and Russell Guest, *Above the Trenches* (Grub Street, London, 1990)

Udet, Ernst, *Ace of the Iron Cross* (Arco Publishing Inc, New York, NY, 1981)

VanWyngarden, Greg, *Osprey Aviation Elite Units 16 – 'Richthofen's Circus' Jagdgeschwader Nr 1* (Osprey Publishing, Oxford, 2004)

VanWyngarden, Greg, *Osprey Aviation Elite Units 19 – Jagdgeschwader Nr II Geschwader Berthold* (Osprey Publishing, Oxford, 2005)

Waugh, Colin, *A Short History of 70 Squadron, RFC/RAF 1916–1919* (Cross & Cockade (USA) Journal, pp.311–312, Vol.20 No.4, Winter 1979)

Whetton, Douglass, *Episodes – an interview with Wing Commander Ronald Adam, OBE,* (Cross & Cockade (USA) Journal, pp.263–268, Vol.13, No.3, Autumn 1972)

INDEX

References to illustrations are shown in **bold**.